HISTORIC
WASHINGTON, DC

HISTORIC WASHINGTON, DC

A Tour of the District's
Top 50 National Landmarks

Lori Wysong

Globe
Pequot
Guilford, Connecticut

Globe
Pequot

An imprint of Globe Pequot, the trade division of The Rowman & Littlefield
Publishing Group, Inc.
4501 Forbes Blvd., Ste. 200
Lanham, MD 20706
www.rowman.com

Distributed by NATIONAL BOOK NETWORK

British Library Cataloguing in Publication Information available

Library of Congress Cataloging-in-Publication Data available

ISBN 978-1-4930-5783-2 (paper: alk. paper)
ISBN 978-1-4930-5784-9 (electronic)

♾™ The paper used in this publication meets the minimum requirements of
American National Standard for Information Sciences—Permanence of Paper for
Printed Library Materials, ANSI/NISO Z39.48–1992.

CONTENTS

GEORGETOWN

PALISADES

DUPONT CIRCLE AND KALORAMA

LOGAN CIRCLE, SHAW, AND HOWARD UNIVERSITY

COLUMBIA HEIGHTS AND UPPER NORTHWEST

NOMA AND NEAR NORTHEAST

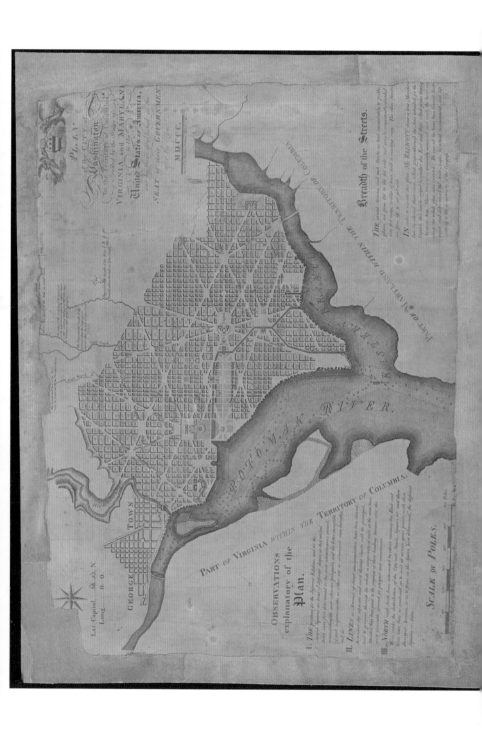

INTRODUCTION

Washington, DC, is a city like no other. It's the political center of one of the most powerful nations in the world, after all. Yet DC is also a city like any other. Though the federal government and bureaucracy impacted the development of the National Historic Landmarks in this book, many of the sites are those you'd find in any city—schools, churches, cemeteries, and private residences. In the case of countless buildings in DC, however, the histories are much more complicated. Private and public life are interwoven as the functions of these sites changed and adapted over time.

Of course, you'll notice a few things in DC's history that were influential on a wide scale. The very formation of the capital city is one of those. Prior to its establishment, the area where DC is today was by no means a naturally budding metropolis. The Nacotchtank Tribe (for whom the Anacostia River is named) had long inhabited the area and used it as a trading post in the seventeenth century. After European settlers displaced them, there were farms and tidal wetlands but no real signs of a fast-growing cityscape. The plans of Pierre Charles L'Enfant, which divided the proposed city into four quadrants and laid out the wide streets connecting federal buildings and monuments, greatly shaped the trajectory of DC's growth. They inspired later architects and planners and directly influenced the McMillan Plan of the early twentieth century, which made the National Mall what we think of today. L'Enfant's meticulous plans, combined with the draw of power and federal jobs, transformed a backwater into a fairly populous capital.

DC has faced challenges unique to the city, like its position as a target for military destruction or the lengthy debates over its level of autonomy and representation. Alongside these challenges, the District encounters many of the same ups and downs as any other city in the country. Yet, because of the heavy political and media presence in Washington, even some local events can come under national and international scrutiny and take on a broader significance.

Through all this, DC has still managed to develop its own local culture, which varies by some of the neighborhoods and even streets where the sites in this book are located. There are 75 National Historic Landmarks in DC, all of which are historically significant, but this guide only contains 50. I selected these sites based primarily on their accessibility to the public and also on their variety of locations and historical and architectural characteristics. The sections in this book are organized by the locations of the sites, so that you can travel fairly easily from the subject of one entry to the next. They span centuries and purposes as well as quadrants and neighborhoods. Still, I regret not being able to include all 75, as each and every one is really worth a visit.

National Historic Landmarks are designated on the basis of their significance pertaining to historic events, exceptional individuals, ideals, architecture, culture, or all of the above. There are a great many buildings not on the list that fit these criteria in some way, shape, or form. Also, as the list used to be limited to buildings 50 years of age or older (and it is still pretty rare to find a newer structure on it), there are a lot of more recent historic sites yet-to-be-designated. I've done my best to allude to a few nearby points of interest in the chapters for some of the sites in this guide, but feel free to go where your intuition takes you! After all, many of the most popular tourist destinations in DC surround the Reflecting Pool, and you won't read about those in here because they are not National Historic Landmarks. Where this guide is useful is that, while the National Historic Landmark list is relatively short, it includes some of the lesser-known sites along with the more famous, which provide a good sense of DC as both an average city and a national capital.

When you visit these sites, remember their story isn't over yet! They will continue to accrue layers of history long after this book is published, and one of the many things that makes these places significant is that there is always more to learn about them.

Library of Congress, see entry on page 5

Congressional Cemetery
**1801 E St. SE, Washington, DC 20003; (202) 543-0539;
congressionalcemetery.org; Open Daily; Free Admission**

Although many visitors to the DC area choose to pay their respects to the illustrious figures interred at Arlington National Cemetery, Congressional Cemetery has been called "American Westminster Abbey" for the famous people buried there and was the national cemetery of the US around 50 years before Arlington Cemetery came into existence.

There was no space allotted for burials in L'Enfant's original design for Washington, DC. By 1807, an association composed mostly of members of the Christ Church who lived near Capitol Hill set out to do something about this blatant lack of cemeteries. They selected four and a half acres for this purpose (today there are over 37) and sold plots to pay off the land and other expenses. People of color and "infidels" were denied burial at this point, so many of the prominent Black figures in other entries (like Charlotte Forten Grimké and Mary Ann Shadd Cary) were buried at the now-defunct Columbian Harmony Cemetery in the U Street Corridor, which was reinterred in Landover, MD, in 1959 and is today the site of the Rhode Island Ave-Brentwood Metro Station. Despite its initial racist and exclusionary practices, Congressional Cemetery grew, and by 1812 its debts were paid off; the graveyard was turned over officially to Christ Church and christened "Washington Parish Burial Ground."

Even before it received its first name, however, Congressional Cemetery had strong ties to the legislative branch. In 1807, Federalist Senator Uriah Tracy was buried there. Over the years, it has been the final resting place of countless congressmen who died in the District and a temporary stop for other politicians and presidents, housing their remains in a receiving vault until they could be transported elsewhere for final burial. For many years, in addition to the tombstones for congressmen actually buried there, Congress erected cenotaphs designed by the second Architect of the Capitol Benjamin Latrobe (whose daughter is also interred at the cemetery) for members of Congress buried elsewhere. It is hard to miss the rows of towering Egyptian-style sandstone monuments erected in their memory (this practice ceased when the cemetery ran out of space for them in 1878). Also check out the chapel, at the axial center of the site, which sometimes hosts events open to the public.

In addition to the various senators and representatives beneath its soil, many notable military leaders and Native American diplomats are buried there, as well as band leader John Philip Sousa and FBI Director J. Edgar Hoover. Near Hoover's grave is what's known as the "gay corner" of the cemetery, where in the 1980s Leonard Matlovich, discharged from the military for his sexual practices, chose to be buried near the FBI leader who targeted gay employees in the federal government in the 1950s and 1960s. Many other LGBT veterans and citizens have since followed in his footsteps and have chosen this corner of the cemetery for interment.

Egyptian-inspired cenotaph for John Quincy Adams, designed by Benjamin Latrobe

The cemetery is active today, with burials and other events like yoga, film screenings, dog walking, and an annual birthday concert for John Philip Sousa every November. This wasn't always the case, though. For many years, the oldest cemetery in the District was untended and neglected, and many headstones were lost (there are about 60,000 people buried there). This situation was remedied only in the late 1990s, when several community volunteer groups formed to maintain and preserve the National Historic Landmark. Despite the cemetery's title, it is not government property but is owned by the nonprofit Association for the Preservation of Historic Congressional Cemetery. If you want to respectfully explore the burial space, an audio tour is available on the cemetery's website, and themed guided tours are given on weekends.

John Philip Sousa Jr. High School
3650 Ely Pl SE, Washington, DC 20019; (202) 729-3260; profiles.dcps.dc.gov/Sousa+Middle+School; Closed to Public

Most people associate the desegregation of public schools in the US with *Brown vs. The Board of Education*, but as this case was being deliberated, another lesser-known Supreme Court case brought the debate straight to the nation's capital.

The court case was born at John Philip Sousa Jr. High School (now a middle school), built to serve local white students, which stands today as a symbol of the unique struggle for Civil Rights in DC.

Soon after it opened in September of 1950, eleven Black students requested and were denied admission to the school, even though there were many empty classrooms that could have welcomed them.

The African American population in DC had increased substantially in the previous decades as new school construction declined during World War II. John Philip Sousa Jr. High was a brand-new postwar school, built in 1950, but there was no such equivalence for DC's Black students, who attended schools that were poorly maintained, overcrowded, and lacking resources.

Because of this gross inequity, the attempt to desegregate John Philip Sousa Jr. High was no random event but was in fact carefully planned since the year before. Howard University law professor and future Howard president James Nabrit Jr., Gardner Bishop (a local barber and Civil Rights activist who had previously tried to improve conditions at his children's middle school), and the Consolidated Parents Group from Anacostia were the brains behind the effort.

The students chosen to break the barrier between "separate-but-equal" schools were accompanied by lawyers and policemen escorting them to the John Philip Sousa Jr. High, but the principal still refused them entry. Among these students was Spottswood Bolling, under whose name the ensuing court case was filed against school superintendent Melvin Sharpe.

Bolling vs. Sharpe was a landmark case that ended "separate-but-equal" school segregation in DC. Charles Hamilton Houston, a Howard University legend (see separate entry) and National Association for the Advancement of Colored People (NAACP) Counsel, died before he could make much progress on the case, and so Nabrit succeeded him. Although the local courts dismissed it due to a previous precedent upholding segregation, Nabrit appealed and the Supreme Court heard the case. While *Brown vs. Board* applied to states based on the equal protection clause of the Fourteenth Amendment (which covers states), the unanimous 1954 *Bolling vs. Sharpe* decision took its legitimacy from the fact that discrimination based on race violated the Fifth Amendment's due process clause (which applies to the federal government and therefore DC).

The two cases were decided at practically the same time and served similar purposes in the quest to desegregate. Just as *Brown vs. Board* was the beginning of the end of segregation in the US, *Bolling vs. Sharpe* marked a similar milestone in the District.

By fall of 1954, schools in DC opened on a desegregated basis, including John Philip Sousa Jr. High. The school has been in operation ever since, now serving students of all colors and backgrounds. It gained National Historic Landmark Status in 2001. If you visit, be aware that this is an active middle school, and the grounds and interior are closed to the public.

Library of Congress
101 Independence Ave SE, Washington, DC 20540; (202) 707-5000; loc.gov; Open Mon through Sat; Free Admission

What we may think of today as a national library for the US was once exactly what its title suggests: a Library of Congress. Its very founding was linked to the capital city itself. When John Adams signed an act of Congress in 1800, moving the capital from Philadelphia to DC, it included a $5,000 allocation for purchasing books specifically for the legislative branch. In 1802, the next president, Thomas Jefferson, appointed the first congressional librarians (the president still appoints the position of head librarian to this day). He also expanded the group allowed to use the new resource to include members of the executive branch. By the 1830s, the library was unofficially available to the public.

The Library of Congress was still a small institution located in the west side of the Capitol when the British burned its first iteration to the ground in 1814, during their occupation of DC in the War of 1812. Due to its governmental supporters, however, the library grew back bigger than ever. Thomas Jefferson allowed Congress to purchase his own personal collection of books to replace those destroyed, asking them to pay whatever they would (some Federalists disapproved, but the purchase ultimately took place).

It would not be the last time the library faced destruction. There was another, albeit smaller, fire at the Capitol in 1825 and a much larger blaze caused by a faulty chimney in 1851 which destroyed two thirds of Jefferson's collection along with the part of the building designed by third Architect of the Capitol, Charles Bulfinch.

The library's section of the Capitol was rebuilt, along with a new, iron fireproof dome added by the fourth Architect of the Capitol, Thomas U. Walter. However, the Library of Congress soon outgrew its home at the Capitol as it became even less exclusive to the government. Ainsworth Rand Spofford, head librarian from 1864 to 1897, transformed it into more of a national institution. As the city and the nation grew after the Civil War, he greatly increased the library's collection and suggested the need for a separate space in 1871.

The result was the Jefferson Building, authorized by Congress in 1886. It is the best known of the library's buildings today and by far the most elaborate, with its

gold-leaf dome, sculptures, lush interior furnishing, and stunning murals. Dozens of artisans worked on the project, which was based on the Paris Opera House.

Once completed, the many books at the old location were transported by the shelf-load to the new building via wooden chutes. When the new library building opened in 1897, the entire public was officially welcome, though underground tunnels with book conveyor belts and pneumatic tubes connected the library to the Capitol so that Congress still had easy access.

Since then, two additional buildings, the Annex Building and the James Madison Memorial Building (also home of the US Copyright Office), were added to the library complex. Researchers from all over the world visit this library once reserved for a select few, which adds more than 10,000 items (books, photos, music—even tweets) to its collections daily. In addition to its grand reading room and labyrinthine hallways, the Jefferson building also hosts exhibits on a variety of topics open to the general public.

Marine Corps Barracks and Commandant's House
801 G St SE, Washington, DC 20390; barracks.marines.mil/ History/Home-of-the-Commandants; Closed to the Public

Many would assume that the White House (see separate entry) holds the record as the oldest continuously used house built for public officials. Yet, in DC, the House of the Commandants actually claims that title. This is no small feat, given that the occupation of the White House and many other federal buildings was disturbed by the destruction of the War of 1812. When the British burned the White House, along with countless other buildings in the capital city, the Commandant's House was spared.

Though there could be many reasons why it escaped destruction, the Marine Corps' preferred legend has to do with the military maneuvers leading up to the burning of the City. At the Battle of Bladensburg, otherwise a failure for the Americans because it allowed the British to creep closer to DC, many Marines and sailors did not receive the order to retreat. Around 500 men were left to stave off the British Forces, taking a two-hour stand that delayed the British long enough for James and Dolley Madison to escape the capital (see White House entry). Was the Commandant's House spared out of respect for the bravery of the US Marines? This seems unlikely, but it would certainly make quite a story.

Even aside from this near miss in 1814, the residence of the Commandant (highest in command for that branch of the military and a member of the Joint Chiefs of Staff) is the oldest building in the oldest continually active post in the Marine Corps, the US Marine Corps Barracks. There was a need for the barracks compound as soon as the Marine Corps came into being.

The origins of the branch stem from 1775 with the formation of the Continental Marines (part of the Continental Army), which disbanded after the Revolutionary War. In 1798, President Adams re-established the Marines as a military branch alongside the army and navy. The Marines headquartered in Philadelphia until 1800, when they moved to DC. President Jefferson and Lt. Col. William Ward Burrows, the second Commandant of the Marine Corps, chose a spot for the base close to the Capitol and Navy Yard and advertised a $100 prize for an architect who could suitably design the Commandant's residence. George Hadfield, who designed the Custis-Lee House, supervised the construction of the Capitol, and would go on to design the DC Courthouse (see separate entries), won the contract for designing the original barracks and Commandant's House.

Construction on the Barracks and Commandant's House under the Jefferson administration lasted from 1801 to 1808. The barracks have mostly been replaced over time, but the house remains. Though the house is one of the oldest continuously occupied public spaces in DC, it doesn't look quite as it did when it was first built. It began as a symmetrical, Federal-style house. Yet additions from later in the nineteenth century created a symmetrical imbalance and added features like mansard roofs and cornices that are more in keeping with Victorian architecture. Today, white paint covers the original Flemish Bond style brickwork of the house, which has been home to all but the first two commandants. The interiors have been modernized and personalized depending on who was inhabiting the house.

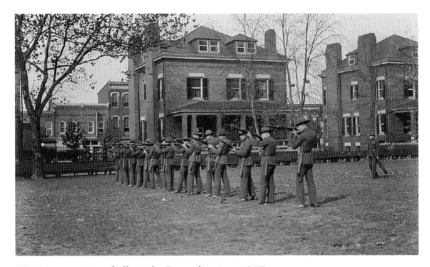

Marines practicing drills at the Barracks, circa 1917

John Philip Sousa, circa 1880–1892

House of the Commandants

Beginning in the early twentieth century (1900–1907), Hadfield's original quadrangle of Barracks received extensive renovation and reconstruction, and though they may not appear as they once did, they too have a rich history. Just like today, there were buildings on the compound for offices, living space, and maintenance facilities. In addition to their exploits in the War of 1812, Marines from these barracks received elite training to fight in other conflicts, from the halls of Montezuma (a factually inaccurate reference to the Mexican American War) to the Shores of Tripoli (First Barbary War). They also played a role in the capture of John Brown at Harpers Ferry, the Civil War, and the Spanish American War. As the US military greatly expanded throughout the nineteenth century, Commandants like Archibald Henderson (from 1820 to 1859) and Charles Heywood (from 1891 to 1903) modified training and tactics, shaping the Corps into what it is today. Though by 1911 this site stopped its recruit training, in more recent history, Marines from these barracks deployed for Operations Desert Shield and Desert Storm.

Along with its significance to US military history, this is a site of huge musical importance. The Marine Corps Band, which began unofficially in the early nineteenth century but became an official institution in 1861, blossomed in the Band Hall of the Barracks. "The March King," John Philip Sousa, took charge of the band from 1880 to 1892 and composed some of his best-known pieces, "Stars and Stripes Forever" and "Semper Fidelis," while here. These barracks are still the home of the Marines' renowned band, and there is even a statue of Sousa on-site.

Just as the band is often found at important civic ceremonies, many of the Marines stationed here today often perform ceremonial duties at local destinations like the White House and Arlington National Cemetery. Due to the continued presence of the Marines here, the Barracks and Commandant's House are not currently open to the public.

Sewall-Belmont House
144 Constitution Ave. NE Washington, DC 20002; (202) 546-1210; nationalwomansparty.org/visit; Open Wed through Sun, Regularly Scheduled Tours Given; Free Admission

A stone's throw from the US Capitol, the Sewall-Belmont House is one of the oldest residential buildings in Washington, DC. The original house was built in 1800, just a decade after the city's founding. Robert Sewall, a prominent Marylander, purchased the property and rented his new home to the Secretary of the Treasury Albert Gallatin (who served in that position for both Jefferson and Madison) soon after its construction.

According to tradition, the British burned down the original house in 1814, when they invaded Washington, DC, during the War of 1812. Sewall rebuilt his home by 1820, and it remained within his family for over a century, until Vermont Senator Porter Dale purchased the property in 1922. While prominent political figures like Senator Dale and Treasury Secretary Gallatin occupied the house, the most famous tenants were those denied the right to political participation.

The National Women's Party (NWP) bought the house in 1929, along with two neighboring rowhouses, to use as its headquarters as well as a dwelling place and hotel for some party members. The NWP had its start in 1913, when suffragist Alice Paul founded it as the "Congressional Union for Women's Suffrage" (the name was officially changed a few years later). The NWP's goal was to gain the support of political parties for women's rights and withhold support from parties in power who did not endorse women's suffrage. The NWP held marches through the streets of DC, and at one point, its famous "silent sentinels" picketed the White House daily. Many NWP members were arrested for their protests, and some used tactics like hunger strikes while they were in prison to bring attention to their cause. The steps from the Occoquan Workhouse, where many of the women were imprisoned, can be seen today next to the Sewall-Belmont House.

The NWP named the house after Alva Belmont, who was president of the Party from 1920 to 1933 and who contributed much of the funds used to purchase the

Steps of the Occoquan Workhouse

house. Since women gained the right to vote in 1920, years before the party bought the property, the goals of the NWP during its time at the Sewall-Belmont House were expanded beyond suffrage. Party members promoted the Equal Rights Amendment (the first version had been drafted by Paul in 1922), seeking equality for women in other facets of American life. The party also engaged with international struggles for women's rights while the house was its headquarters.

At certain moments, NWP members also had to fight for the house itself. In the late 1960s and early 1970s, there were several attempts by congressmen to confiscate the house so that a new Senate office building (or a driveway leading there) could be built. Thankfully, these efforts were resisted by party members, including Alice Paul.

More recent politicians have recognized the significance of the site to women's history. It was declared a national monument for women's equality in 2016, in addition to its National Historic Landmark status.

The house still serves as NWP headquarters, although the organization today is mostly focused on educating about the women's rights movement. The house museum features important artifacts, including busts of famous women's rights advocates, protest banners, and other memorabilia from the suffrage movement, such as Susan B. Anthony's desk and Elizabeth Cady Stanton's chair. As you take in these unique objects, also observe the rooms they are displayed in. The architecture of the brick house reflects the changing tastes in home design over the centuries.

Supreme Court Building
1 First St., NE Washington, DC 20543; (202) 479-3000; supremecourt.gov/about/courtbuilding.aspx; Open Mon through Fri; Free Admission

The Supreme Court represents the judicial branch of the US government, so we might assume that the building that houses it is as old as the White House or the Capitol (see separate entries). In fact, it was built in 1935, and prior to that point the Supreme Court met in the Capitol building.

After its first meeting in 1790, the Supreme Court met briefly in New York and later at Philadelphia's Independence Hall and City Hall when that city was the nation's capital. As the capital moved to DC in 1800, the court moved with it. The justices convened in various rooms of the Capitol, but because the legislative building was very much a work in progress (a fire set by the British partially destroyed it during the War of 1812), the justices were frequently displaced by construction and had to meet in nearby taverns and houses.

The impetus for a permanent home did not come until William Howard Taft decided to do something about it. In 1929, he argued that the Supreme Court deserved its own space to distance itself from Congress as a separate branch of government. Though he was Chief Justice of the Supreme Court at the time, Taft began this campaign years before in 1912 while he was still head of the executive branch as president.

All branches were involved in creating the building: Taft headed a commission created by Congress to oversee the project. A site along First Street close to Union Station was selected for the building. Cass Gilbert, who was behind the design of several American skyscrapers, came aboard as the architect. His design was meant to echo the historic traditions of other government buildings. He used classical motifs and Corinthian pillars and made the building deliberately smaller and less imposing than its more contemporary federal structures. The temple-like exterior concealed a grand interior space with dark marble floors, cantilevered marble staircases, and several courtyards dividing the various sections of the building.

Unfortunately, Taft did not live to see the cornerstone laid. Construction began in 1932, two years after his death, but his successors considered the building his final legacy. Gilbert, too, died before his work was completed and his son oversaw the largely mahogany furnishing of the courtrooms. Though he intended it as an elegant and dignified space, some thought it too gaudy or ostentatious.

Gilbert's design incorporated large quantities of marble from Vermont, Georgia, and Alabama used in various components of the structure. The western facade displays an elaborate sculptural program, including a pediment with the figures Liberty, Order, and Authority; the slogan "Equal Justice Under Law"; and the famous seated figures enclosing the stairway, "Contemplation of Justice" and "Authority of Law" by James Earle Fraser (sculptor of many other statues associated with DC's government buildings). The lesser-known east side of the building contains a pediment

Cantilevered marble staircase, Supreme Court interior

centering famous lawmakers Moses, Confucius, and Solon above the slogan "Justice the Guardian of Liberty."

This view of the building as excessive was probably augmented by the fact that the bulk of its construction took place in the midst of the Great Depression; there were even some delays due to labor strikes. Today, however, the building is a representation of the principles of justice and equality. Too many landmark cases to name have been decided beneath its roof since the court first convened there in October of 1935.

As you walk through the halls, a number of faces will stare down at you—a bust of every previous Supreme Court justice to be exact. Say hello to Taft, if you like. If you do visit, be sure to check the Court's daily calendar online to make sure that the Supreme Court's official business isn't impacting visiting hours.

United States Capitol
US Capitol Visitor Center, US Capitol, East Capitol St. NE, First St. SE, Washington, DC 20004; (202) 226-8000; visitthecapitol. gov; Open Mon through Sat; Free Admission

No building is as central to the plans for Washington, DC, as the US Capitol. It lies at the intersection of the city's four geographical quadrants, making the legislative branch a centerpiece of the city and a global symbol. Though we might think of it as a fixed, iconic structure, it underwent (and continues to undergo) countless changes and iterations.

Pierre Charles L'Enfant, who planned the city's physical space, was supposed to design the Capitol as well but lost his job over conflicts with the DC commissioners. The design of the enormous project was thus put forth as a nationwide contest. The winning entry ended up arriving after the entry period closed, from a Scottish doctor living in the British West Indies. Dr. William Thornton became the first Architect of the Capitol with a neoclassical design of two wings connecting to a low dome at the center.

George Washington laid the cornerstone for Thornton's plan in 1793, and the long project of building the Capitol was begun. Dr. Thornton was an amateur architect, and so in the earliest years, several other architects oversaw the building of his design, including James Hoban, designer of the White House (see separate entry), who was in charge of the construction of the north wing (today home to the Senate). Much of the physical labor in these early years was done by local enslaved people. Today, Emancipation Hall at the Capitol Visitor Center is named to acknowledge and honor their contributions to constructing the Capitol.

Construction paused for a time until Benjamin Latrobe took over as second Architect of the Capitol in 1803, adding office and meeting space to Thornton's south wing (today home to the House of Representatives) and a Supreme Court chamber (see separate entry) to the north wing. Latrobe was also responsible in large part for overseeing the rebuilding process after the British destroyed the original Capitol construction in 1814 (a rainstorm saved it from complete incineration) until 1818, when the third Architect of the Capitol Charles Bulfinch largely continued with previous designs and made the central dome a bit taller to better fit the proportions of the structure.

Though incomplete, the Capitol Building sufficiently served its purposes in the early nineteenth century, but as the country expanded and more and more states

Capitol Freedom Statue

joined the Union, the growing legislative branch needed more space. Yet another competition was held to determine the fourth Architect of the Capitol Thomas Ustick Walter, who created a large expansion with extra wings and terraces designed by Frederick Law Olmsted. Walter monitored this fairly rapid construction, which was mostly complete by the late 1850s. Of course, the massive expansion caused Bulfinch's dome to look disproportionately tiny, but nothing could be done about this until construction resumed after the Civil War.

In the meantime, the Capitol was used as a military hospital, barracks, and even a bakery before construction continued in 1862. It was during this era that the Capitol gained some of its trademark adornments. The bronze "Statue of Freedom" sculpture by Thomas Crawford was placed atop the dome in 1863, after the fifth Architect of the Capitol Edward Clark completed an expansion of it. It was also in the 1860s that Constantino Brumidi painted Vatican-inspired masterworks, like the famous Apotheosis of Washington in the rotunda and the murals on the walls of the Senate wing (known as the Brumidi corridors).

Modern conveniences like elevators, heating, and even bathtubs for the congressmen and their families were installed in the second half of the nineteenth century. The Library of Congress and Supreme Court (see separate entries), which had been housed there, moved out in the late nineteenth and early twentieth centuries, leaving more room for a still-growing Congress. Later architects updated the building with fireproofing and interior renovations; this would come in handy, as fires were a constant in Capitol history and there were at least two bombing attempts on the Capitol in the twentieth century alone. At the same time as it was modernizing, restorations were also taking place. Leading up to the Nation's Bicentennial, projects of reinforcement and conservation, which lasted several decades in various iterations, were used to preserve and highlight some of the building's original fabric.

The Capitol exemplifies how one building can reflect many changes in a city and also in federal government. The structure has adapted to wars, a growing Congress, and changing technologies. As the latter has made government actions more transparent to the public, so also has the building itself become more accessible. Today, the new Capitol Visitor Center showcases the storied history of the building and the branch of government it houses. Visitors can see the statues representing each state, the crypt with columns supporting the Capitol dome, and the rotunda where so many prominent American figures have lain in state before burial. Though same-day passes are available at the Information Desk on the lower level, if you visit, it may be easier to schedule in advance online or through your Senator or Representative's office.

Washington Navy Yard
11th and O St. gate (Main Entrance), Washington Navy Yard, Washington, DC 20003; (202) 433-3738; cnic.navy.mil/regions/ ndw/installations/nsa_washington.html; Open Mon through Fri; Free Admission

The Washington Navy Yard, the first US naval hub along the shore, was established in 1799 when the US Navy was regenerated after a few decades of dormancy following the American Revolution. This initial home base for the navy, as well as the operations it housed, contributed to the US growth as a global military power.

In its earliest days, the Navy Yard was a center for shipbuilding, but it has changed a great deal in size and function since that time. This is in no small part due to the fact that it burned to the ground during the War of 1812, though it wasn't technically destroyed by British invasion of DC in 1814. The destruction of the Navy Yard was part of a scorched-earth tactic that incinerated all but a single schooner, the barracks, a few offices, and the quarters of Commandant Thomas Tingey, the man who ordered the fire.

The main gate, today often known as the Latrobe gate for its creator, is another survivor of the fire. In addition to his many architectural achievements in the District and elsewhere, Benjamin Latrobe served as the official Engineer of the Navy Department after 1804. He designed the overall plan for the Navy Yard, as well as the recognizable entranceway.

Today, this gate, along with the other extant buildings from before the fire, can be seen by visitors to the Navy Yard, though many of the oldest structures look remarkably different from their original forms.

These changes are understandable; as the Navy Yard itself evolved over time, so did its buildings. After the War of 1812, military officials realized that it might make more sense to move ship-making functions closer to the ocean, so the compound became a site of manufacturing for naval equipment. In subsequent wars, it escaped the excitement of battle, but played an important role nonetheless, especially once the Confederacy captured the Norfolk Navy Yard in 1861. Ships like the ironclad *Monitor* were repaired in DC, and the Navy Yard was responsible for maintaining the *Potomac Flotilla*, which defended the river from enemy advances. Following the Lincoln assassination in 1865, John Wilkes Booth's body was examined at a ship docked at the Navy Yard.

As naval technology continued to advance in the decades after the Civil War, the primary focus of the Navy Yard became making ordnances, used successfully against the Spanish in the late 1890s to make the US a world power with colonial holdings. Production continued at various levels throughout the early twentieth century in accord with the arms limitations treaties of the 1920s, and the great demand brought on by World Wars I and II. In the 1940s, it became the largest naval ordnance plant in the world, when many men and women toiled in the factories to make weapons to be sent overseas. Weapon design, research, and testing became the focus after the War, when the Navy Yard was temporarily renamed the "United States Naval Gun Factory."

By 1962, however, naval technology shifted from big gunships to submarines and other newer advances, and the Navy Yard's factory closed, leaving other plants to manufacture weapons. Today, it is an administrative center for the navy, and a destination for history lovers. Not only does the Navy Yard have its own museum and

Latrobe Gate

several nationally registered historic sites (mostly the pre–War of 1812 structures), it is also the docking site of the Presidential Yacht, the USS *Sequoia*, which is another National Historic Landmark.

If you visit, security is understandably tighter than some of the other historic sites. The Navy Yard was the target of a mass shooting in 2013, and as a military facility it may require you to complete a form in advance, have a felony-free record, and bring your driver's license or other identification with you. It's a good idea to call ahead for details.

Pension Building, see entry on page 31

JUDICIARY SQUARE AND PENN QUARTER

City Hall/DC Courthouse
430 E St. NW, #115, Washington, DC 20001; (202) 879-2700;
dccourts.gov/court-of-appeals/historic-courthouse; Closed to Public

One of the earliest municipal buildings in the nation's capital, the first version of this structure was the DC City Hall, built beginning in 1820. The city government held a competition to determine who would design the structure. The winning architect, George Hadfield, famously designed several other DC area sites throughout his career, including the original Treasury Building, the Marine Corps Commandant's House, and the Arlington House (Custis-Lee Mansion). Because of inconsistent funding, an ultimately scaled-down version of Hadfield's very grand plan was not completed until 1849.

In its earliest decades, the building held a number of offices, including the US Circuit Court, Register of Wills, DC Supreme Court, Orphan's Court, and DC Police Headquarters. Many notable figures have worked within its walls, including Francis Scott Key, who as a District Attorney held his office there in the 1830s and 1840s, and Frederick Douglass, who served as US Marshal for the District in 1877. Teddy Roosevelt worked in the west wing of the building from 1889 to 1895 during his stint with the Civil Service Commission.

The courthouse is just as famous for the high-profile cases that were tried here, including the much-publicized Teapot Dome Scandal. Perhaps more intriguing are the assassins who faced trial in this courthouse. In 1835, Andrew Jackson's would-be assassin Richard Lawrence was acquitted here for his unsuccessful attempt on the grounds of insanity. Charles Guiteau, the man who assassinated President Garfield, was not so fortunate. He was tried here before the District Supreme Court in 1882 and pled insanity, but the jury was unconvinced and convicted Guiteau of his crime.

Probably the most famous trial that occurred here took place in the summer of 1867. John Surratt Jr. was implicated in the conspiracy to assassinate Abraham Lincoln because of his previous plans with John Wilkes Booth to kidnap the president. He received a civil trial in the building with a jury that could not agree on a verdict.

One year later, on the third anniversary of Lincoln's assassination, the large statue you see in front of the courthouse was dedicated. The famous portrayal of Lincoln was created by Lot Flannery, an Irish immigrant who made a career of stone carving in Washington, DC. Flannery personally knew President Lincoln and was present at Ford's Theatre the night he was shot.

You've probably noticed that the courthouse behind the statue does not look like it's from the nineteenth century, and that's quite a story. A few nineteenth-century additions and renovations were made aside from Hadfield's design, but in 1916, the entire courthouse was reinforced with concrete and steel. This meant that almost all of the original architectural fabric of the building was stripped away, and the courthouse was renovated using largely new materials. In 1999, the building prepared for another renovation, this time taking 10 years. Because the 1916 renovators never bothered to rebuild the north-facing portico, twenty-first-century architects conceived a portico of glass and steel in dialogue with the building's past. Aside from this obviously modern element, the renovation preserved the building's original fabric and restored its interiors as much as possible. Only the exterior of the courthouse is open for the public to view, however, as the building currently houses the highest municipal court in the nation's capital, the DC Court of Appeals.

General Post Office
700 F St. NW, Washington, DC 20004; (202) 628-7177; monaco-dc.com; Lobby Open to Public Daily; Free Admission

The General Post Office, like many federal buildings, has served differing and versatile purposes over the years. In the early nineteenth century, two federal offices, the Patent Office (see separate entry) and the Post Office, shared the same space. When the British destroyed several federal buildings by fire in the War of 1812, these two offices (along with Congress) temporarily moved into a local building called Blodgett's Hotel. After Blodgett's itself burned to the ground in 1836, it became clear that both agencies would need a new home.

President Andrew Jackson chose architect Robert Mills, who went on to design the Washington Monument, to design both the General Post Office and Patent Office (along with the Treasury Building, see separate entry). Of the three, Mills considered the General Post Office his best work. Built on the same site as Blodgett's Hotel, the Post Office was to be enormous (today it appears even more so because as the street levels were lowered over time, the basement became more visible). Mills chose classical marble as the chief material for the restrained building (it's the first structure in DC entirely made of the pearly stone), which echoes the Patent Office in its alternation between porticoes and pilasters along the sides of the building. The elegant Corinthian columns contrast somewhat with the imposing, less frivolous Doric style of the Patent Office. The Post Office is heavily influenced by Roman and Italianate temples as well as Renaissance styles.

Construction was completed on the Post Office in 1842, and early on it housed important activities aside from the typical snail mail we might think of from that period. In 1845, for example, Samuel Morse operated the first Public Telegraph Office in the US out of the building, and a plaque on 7th Street commemorates his efforts today.

As the bureaucratic organization it housed expanded, the already large building became even larger. None other than fourth Architect of the Capitol Thomas Ustick Walter expanded on Mill's original design beginning in 1855. Walter incorporated iron joists to support his archways, a precursor to steel-frame construction that was ahead of its time. Except for a few minor details, he stayed true to his predecessor's vision (if you want to compare, Mills' section faces E Street and extends onto part of 7th and 8th Streets in a U Shape). Like many other projects, the extension was put on hold due to the Civil War, when troops used the basement as a munitions depot, but it was finally completed in 1866.

As the ever-expanding Post Office prepared to relocate to the "Old Post Office" (later the Trump International Hotel), a new agency moved into the General Post Office in 1897. The General Land Office (GLO), which oversaw the sale and surveying of public lands (particularly in the western US), moved in for a time until 1921; a few years later the US Tariff Commission took its place there.

Despite its federal, historical, and architectural significance (and its National Historic Landmark status as of 1971), the building remained vacant for decades after the Tariff Commission, which became the International Trade Commission in 1974, left in 1988. Maintenance and pest control lagged, and the building soon became a fit home for little more than the rodents that sheltered there. For a time, the Smithsonian considered taking it over, but as talks ensued, nothing was done to repair the building.

Finally, the General Services Administration (GSA) held a contest for ideas to revitalize the structure, and in 2002 the winning proposal was realized. Today, the building serves as the luxury Hotel Monaco, which has attempted to preserve many aspects of Mills's luxury interiors and furnish the rooms in a manner compatible with the building's long and winding history. Today, visitors can step into the lobby to get a sample of these interiors, or maybe even stop for a meal in the hotel's restaurant and courtyard. The building represents an alternative preservation use from the museum or historic house model, and at the same time it is different from those buildings that still serve their original purpose like houses, churches, and federal agencies.

Old Patent Office Building
(Smithsonian National Portrait Gallery and Museum of American Art)

8th and F Sts. NW, Washington, DC 20001; (202) 633-8300 (NPG); (202) 633-7970 (SAAM); npg.si.edu; americanart.si.edu; Open Daily; Free Admission

In L'Enfant's original design for Washington, DC, the place where the Old Patent Office now stands was designated as a "church of the Republic." This grand Greek

Revival building, conceived by architect Robert Mills with a portico based on the Parthenon in Athens, was initially intended as a nondenominational place of worship for the nation's new capital.

Instead, it became known as a "temple to the industrial arts," housing the country's newest innovations. DC's original patent office was destroyed in a fire in 1836, the same year that construction of the new building was begun. Although the structure was not officially completed until 1868, the Patent Office moved into the building in 1842. It granted patents there for nearly a century, until 1932, at which point the office became a space for the Civil Service Commission (today known as the Office of Personnel Management).

The Patent Office served far more crucial purposes than housing federal offices, however. During the Civil War, it was converted into a temporary barracks, a hospital, and a morgue for Union soldiers. Clara Barton notably volunteered as one of the nurses at the hospital, and Walt Whitman came by frequently to read to and talk with the wounded patients.

As the war neared its end, the Patent Office was used for more festive activities. On March 6, 1865, Abraham Lincoln hosted his second Inaugural Ball there. Around 4,000 attendees enjoyed an evening of lively dancing and a sumptuous buffet, which by the end of the boisterous night was trampled on the floor by rowdy guests.

Foreshadowing its current purpose as the home of the Smithsonian American Art Museum and the National Portrait Gallery, more than half of the Old Patent Office was originally designated as an exhibit space in the nineteenth century. The Declaration of Independence, Ben Franklin's printing press, and a piece of Plymouth Rock were among the artifacts housed there, along with the collection of the National Institute (a forerunner of the Smithsonian Institution). In those days, anyone seeking a patent was required to submit scale miniatures of their invention to the office, so a sizeable number of patent models were also on display there. Thousands of these were unfortunately destroyed in an 1877 fire, though many of the most significant were rescued by staff. The building survived the blaze, but the west and north wings were severely damaged and later rebuilt in Victorian style (especially noticeable in the elaborate Great Hall on the third floor).

The Old Patent Office was threatened with destruction again in the 1950s, this time with demolition. Thankfully, it was spared when Congress decided to give the building to the Smithsonian Institution in 1962. After a restoration of the space, it opened to the public in 1968 as the National Portrait Gallery and the American Art Museum. Today, the building that houses these two museums is officially known as the Donald W. Reynolds Center for American Art and Portraiture.

Explore both of the museums that now inhabit this space. Make your way through the famous Hall of Presidents at the National Portrait Gallery, climb the ornate staircase to the Luce Foundation Center at the Museum of American Art, and take a break in the Kogod Courtyard at the center of the building. In a gesture to the past life of the museum, some of the surviving nineteenth-century patent models are still on display in the hallways of the first floor.

Kogod Courtyard

Pension Building
401 F St. NW, Washington, DC 20001; (202) 272-2448;
nbm.org; Open Daily; Free Admission

Created by and for veterans, the enormous red-brick Pension Building is one of the grandest structures in DC constructed in the wake of the US Civil War.

It was built to store historic documents and house the Pension Bureau, which doled out money to veterans of prior US conflicts and their families. This massive Italianate Renaissance Revival hall was perhaps meant to represent the rebirth of the US after its largest and most gruesome war yet. Its colorful and elaborate exterior, compounded with the maze-like arcades, made it stand out among other simpler, marble, neoclassical federal structures. Skeptics called it "the Old Red Barn." Prior to the Civil War, most pensions were paid by the states, but amidst a flood of new claims after this critical moment in US history, a federal institution was established to take care of it.

The exterior frieze of Civil War sailors and soldiers, a testament to that conflict's influence on the purpose and design of the structure, is one of the most visible and well-known tributes to Civil War veterans created during their lifetime. Bohemian (from modern day Czechia) artist Caspar-Buberl designed the 1,200-foot terra cotta frame around the outside of the Bureau. Depicting the victorious Union Army, this sculptural relief with Parthenon aspirations suggested the prominence of the American military in society and in government.

This military allusion was no coincidence, as former Union Army Quartermaster General Montgomery C. Meigs (also responsible for the Washington Aqueduct and several other DC structures, see separate entries) designed the Pension Building in 1881, drawing his influence from Italian palaces. At the time it was completed in 1887, the Corinthian columns in the structure's great hall were among the tallest in the world, and the building itself was the largest brick structure at the time of its completion. It was Meigs's last commission before his death in 1892 and was such a lavish setting for federal bureaucracy that several inaugural balls, for presidents Cleveland, McKinley, Theodore Roosevelt, Taft, and Nixon, were held here over the years.

The building is also noteworthy for its technological innovation. Meigs designed it to withstand DC's hot and muggy summers in a time long before air conditioning, adding a system of air vents and an upward flow of air that would eventually leave the building through the dazzling skylights. He designed the shallow, yet lofty staircases of the building with wounded veterans in mind.

With all of these engineering feats, it seems fitting that today the structure serves as the National Building Museum, which features exhibits and programs on architecture, engineering, and landscape design. Its future was not always so secure, however.

In 1926, the Pension Bureau found a new home in the Department of the Interior Building, at which point the General Accounting Office and eventually a long line of other government offices moved in. The building fell into disrepair and was nearly demolished before its preservation in 1978 and restoration in the 1980s. Today, its visibly red-brick presence in DC's white marble landscape highlights the physical legacy of Civil War veterans and the federal government in the late nineteenth century in a very distinctive way.

Smithsonian Arts and Industries Building, see entry on page 35

Smithsonian Institution Arts and Industries Building
900 Jefferson Dr. SW, Washington, DC 20560; (202) 633-1000;
aib.si.edu; Site Is Scheduled to Reopen in 2021

Though it wasn't the first Smithsonian building on the Mall (the Smithsonian Institution Building was there before it, see separate entry), the Arts and Industries Building was the first structure built there to serve specifically and exclusively as a museum.

Joseph Henry, the first Smithsonian Secretary, did not care much for collecting and exhibiting objects, but his assistant Spencer Fullerton Baird certainly did. Baird eventually replaced Henry as Secretary in 1878, and his interest in ornithology and nature led him to expand the size of the Institution's holdings, which were mostly natural history objects at this time. This inspiration may also have been part of a general trend of exhibitions throughout the US during this time. It was just after the national centennial in Philadelphia, which donated several of its displays to the Smithsonian as well as some money to the new museum's construction. The country was intent on showcasing its growth into a nation that valued learning and culture, and once the collection outgrew the Smithsonian Castle's limited space, the Arts and Industries Building became part of this goal.

Before Joseph Henry died, Baird persuaded him to ask Congress to fund a new museum space. More recent Smithsonian museums, like the National Museum of African American History and Culture and the National Museum of the American Indian, took into account the architecture and art of particular cultures in their designs. Adolf Cluss and Paul Schulze, the architects of the Arts and Industries Building, studied European museum spaces as influences for their structure. The late-Victorian building is officially Romanesque revival: symmetrical, with a floorplan in the shape of a Greek cross. However, it drew from a number of popular cultural influences, with elements like the colorful tilework and exterior brickwork inspired by Islamic culture, as well as Greek and Byzantine influences. Construction began in 1879, and after the 1865 fire at the Smithsonian Castle, the architects decided that fireproof materials like brick and steel would be the best course.

General Montgomery Meigs supervised the buildings structural system and oversaw the project by serving on the National Museum Building Commission, along with Baird and William Tecumseh Sherman, among others. George Brown Goode, a theorist on American museums, visited museums in Europe for inspiration not only for the building's layout but also for its purpose. His goal was to have a museum more focused on education than previous displays that were geared toward public entertainment.

The building opened to the public in 1881, with exhibits on zoology, geology, art, technology, history, and anthropology displayed in mahogany cases. There were objects owned by George Washington, alongside countless taxidermied animals and skeletons. Before any of these displays were installed, however, the site hosted Chester A. Arthur's inaugural ball.

At this point, it was called the old US National Museum Building and was only renamed the Arts and Industries Building in 1910, when its natural history collections were moved to a new site at what is today the National Museum of Natural History, and the building shifted its collection more toward history and technology. This was the original home of the Spirit of St. Louis, the Star-Spangled Banner, and the first lady dresses. These are just a few of the pieces housed here that seeded other future museums, like the Air and Space Museum and the American History Museum.

As new museums were gradually built and the Arts and Industries collections divided into new homes, the building displayed the original gifts from the 1876 centennial in an exhibit on the hundredth anniversary of that exhibition. Unfortunately, the building fell into disrepair over the course of the following decades, until a snowstorm in 2003 damaged the roof so badly that the Arts and Industries Building was

The interior of the Arts and Industries Building undergoing renovations

closed for repairs until it partially reopened in 2015. Today, it houses temporary exhibits and hosts special events on occasion. Its future purpose is still relatively uncertain. If you visit, be sure to check out the nearby carousel and the beautiful Folger Rose Garden adjoining it.

Smithsonian Institution Building
1000 Jefferson Dr. SW, Washington, DC 20560; (202) 633-1000; si.edu/museums/smithsonian-institution-building; Open Daily; Free Admission

The Smithsonian Castle, as it is probably better known, fulfilled desires of political leaders like John Quincy Adams in DC's earliest days as the nation's political capital, who harbored expectations that it would become a cultural capital as well. DC made other attempts to establish centers of museums and learning, such as the Columbian Institute and the National Institution, but none came close to the success that the Smithsonian Institution had after its founding in 1846.

The principal donor that made the Smithsonian possible was James Smithson, an English chemist and mineralogist who believed that knowledge and scientific study bettered society. He willed more than $500,000, his entire fortune, to a country he had never visited to promote the "increase & diffusion of knowledge among men." In the Institution's earliest years, many debates took place over how Smithson's intentions could best be fulfilled. Joseph Henry, the Smithsonian's first Secretary, saw it as an institute for scientific research more than a system of museums and as an organization of national rather than local importance.

In fact, when the Smithsonian Institution Building was being constructed, Henry slowed the process to save more building money to go toward research aims rather than to the elaborate structure. It was finally finished in 1855.

Architect James Renwick Jr. won a contest to design the Smithsonian's first building in 1846, after the Institution's initial founding. It was one of his earlier buildings, but it shaped the trajectory of his career; he went on to design St. Patrick's Cathedral in New York City in 1853 and the Renwick Gallery of the Smithsonian American Art Museum (see separate entry) a few years later.

The Smithsonian board of regents requested a Romanesque structure, typically made of light-colored stone with rounded arches. Renwick, however, incorporated local materials, like the red sandstone from Seneca Creek, Maryland, as well as many European elements, weaving in Gothic components (which were very en-vogue in the Victorian era) and aspects of English Saxon and Norman castles. Because he viewed it as a rather frivolous building, Henry referred to it sardonically as "The Norman Castle" when he first arrived at his post.

Yet, he and his family stayed in the castle's east wing during his tenure as Smithsonian Secretary. At the time, the building was cut off from the rest of DC by a now-defunct canal, though today it is a prominent site on the National Mall. Along with the eventual removal of the canal and creation of the Mall as we know it, there were quite a few other changes to the castle and its landscape. It began as a very all-purpose building for the Smithsonian; during this time, it housed exhibits, administration, libraries, laboratories, specimen storage, and included a space set aside for visiting lecturers and scholars to stay at the Institution.

Unfortunately, much of the building and its contents were lost when the castle burst into flames in 1865. The east wing was later fireproofed in 1884 and ultimately restored to its original castle-like appearance in the late 1960s before becoming a National Historic Landmark in 1977.

The residents of the castle weren't always humans, of course. Spencer F. Baird, Smithsonian secretary beginning in 1878, was among the staff of the Institution who studied owls, and as a result, many of the winged creatures were allowed their free reign of the castle tower until well into the 1950s.

While the Smithsonian has become a national institution that draws visitors from all over the world, its museums and National Zoo are perhaps better known than its ongoing research endeavors. The Smithsonian continues to attract scholars from many fields to study and reside in Washington, DC.

Today, the castle serves as an administrative center for the Smithsonian, with a few exhibits. James Smithson, who never set foot in the US in life, today lies buried in a chapel near the north entrance of the building that began his legacy, as inventor Alexander Graham Bell arranged to transport his body there in 1904.

Philadelphia (US Gundelo) at the National Museum of American History
Constitution Ave. NW, Between 12th and 14th Sts. Washington, DC; (202) 633-3717; americanhistory.si.edu/exhibitions/ gunboat-philadelphia; Open Daily; Free Admission

While most sites on the National Register of Historic Places stay in the same spot, the US gundelo *Philadelphia* is most famous for its adventures traveling on the high seas—or rather, Lake Champlain. This vessel is the only surviving gunboat from the American Revolution and played an important role in the outcome of the war.

The *Philadelphia* was among the first ships created in the colonies for the war's naval efforts, part of a fleet authorized by the Continental Congress that was constructed in present-day Whitehall, New York, in the summer of 1776. Though the wooden gundelo (a flat-bottom sailing barge with the modern spelling "gundalow") is 54 feet long and weighs 29 tons, it may seem rather small and low-tech by the standards of modern military watercraft. Even at the time it was built, the American fleet that the gunboat was part of wasn't exactly state-of-the-art compared to its competition.

The *Philadelphia* faced the British Navy, then one of the strongest in the world, just a few months after its construction. In the summer and fall of 1776, it was one of the ships under the command of none other than Brigadier General Benedict Arnold (still loyal to the colonies during this time, of course) to protect Lake Champlain from an advancing British fleet. Around 44 men, most from the colony of New Hampshire, manned the ship.

On October 11, 1776, in what is today known as the Battle of Valcour Bay, the crew of the *Philadelphia* helped to hold off the British at a narrow strait between Valcour Island and the New York mainland. Cannon fire ultimately struck the *Philadelphia*, causing it to sink after a few hours to the depths of Lake Champlain. The rest of the American fleet didn't fare so well either, and in the end, the superior numbers and firepower of the British won the day. Within two days of the naval battle, they took complete control of Lake Champlain.

Though the short-term outcome seemed dismal, in the long-term the contributions of the *Philadelphia* and other gunboats like it proved very important. The delay of the British Navy gave the American colonists time to prepare for future battles, such as Saratoga, which ended in victory.

Despite its significance, the *Philadelphia* lay forgotten at the bottom of the lake for over a century. Finally, in 1935, civil engineer Lorenzo Haggluend discovered the ship at the lake bottom, along with a 24-pound cannonball that led to its demise in 1776, a few of the ship's own guns, and various other artifacts. These were raised to the surface to be displayed along Lake Champlain and the Hudson River, and eventually at Exeter, New York. For many years, visitors to the New York exhibit could see the ship, complete with cannonball holes, remarkably well-preserved during its stay below the lake's frigid waters.

Haggluend left the *Philadelphia* to the Smithsonian in his will, however, so in 1961 the gunboat made a transition to Washington, DC. The Smithsonian National Museum of American History, founded in 1964, has been its home for many years now. Today, the gunboat is displayed on the third floor of the museum. Examine the boat itself and check out the exhibit about its revolutionary history and 1935 recovery, including artifacts that were found years later on the sunken ship.

White House, see entry on page 80

American Red Cross National Headquarters

430 17th St. NW, Washington, DC 20006; (202) 303-4233; redcross.org/about-us/who-we-are/history.html; Open Wed through Fri; Free Tours Available by Appointment

Many people visit DC to make pilgrimages to its several War Memorials. But apart from the ones by the Reflecting Pool is a lesser-known spot dedicated to the "Heroic Women of the Civil War."

The Vermont-marble Beaux Arts building you see today was constructed from 1915 to 1917, but the organization it houses has a longer history.

The American Red Cross itself was founded in 1881 (in Washington, DC, as a matter of fact), years after the Civil War. Clara Barton based the organization on a global movement that began in Switzerland in the 1860s. The "Angel of the Battlefield" had cared for sick and wounded Union Troops in the US prior to visiting Europe after the War. There, she learned that the Geneva Convention of 1864 granted protection to those wounded in battle and decreed a red cross as a neutral emblem protecting those who ministered to them.

In the US, Congress finally granted the Red Cross its first congressional charter in 1900 and another one five years later, but by that time Barton and her cohort had already assisted in several wars, provided disaster relief, and lobbied for the Global Red Cross to deliver peacetime assistance (something the European Red Cross was slower to adopt).

Though Barton resigned from her post as president (at age 83) over a decade before the construction of the DC headquarters, the space reflects her influence on the Red Cross. For one thing, many of her personal items are on display inside. For another, motifs like faith, hope, and charity (which the Red Cross seeks to provide) are visible throughout the headquarters, from the busts of the three virtues by sculptor Hiram Powers to their appearances as three women in a Tiffany window of St. Filomena donated by the Women's Relief Corps of the North. Because the building was (at the time quite controversially) dedicated to women who helped the wounded on both sides of the Civil War, another window depicting a story of the Faerie Queen was given by the United Daughters of the Confederacy. Both organizations contributed to the third, central window, which depicts a knight with a Red

Cross banner. Emphasizing the neutrality of the organization, they were the largest Tiffany windows commissioned for a nonreligious structure.

Like so many structures in DC, the Red Cross Headquarters has the atmosphere of a secular neoclassical temple. Its design by architects Trowbridge and Livingston made copious use of Vermont marble and Corinthian pillars on the exterior. This was no coincidence, as the building figured into Senator McMillan's plans for the city as a whole. It is for this reason that it faces the Ellipse, with views across the meticulously planned green space.

Today, the building still serves as an office space for the American Red Cross, which since the time it was built has grown and helped victims of wars, national disasters, and terrorist attacks, not to mention established its civilian blood collection program. These various efforts have led to additional commemorations at the site, like the statue of the founder of the Red Cross Nursing Service, Jane Delano, which is dedicated to Delano and the many other nurses who died in World War I. Another statue in the sculpture garden depicts Red Cross members assisting a fallen soldier and is dedicated generally to all Red Cross members who gave their lives serving the Red Cross.

The building also functions as a museum of the organization, which offers free tours to visitors. As the Red Cross Headquarters is a working office space, tours are available by reservation, and visitors may need to bring identification or be subject to other security screening.

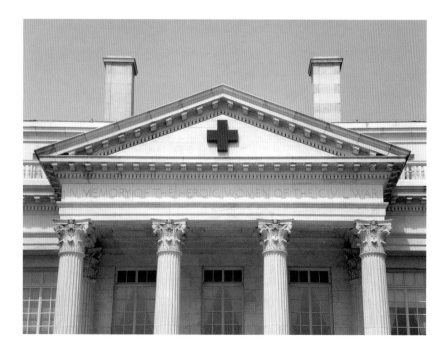

A memorial to Jane Delano at the Red Cross Headquarters

Ashburton House
**1525 H St. NW, Washington, DC 20005; stjohns-dc.org/
welcome-to-saint-johns-church/history; Closed to Public**

Lafayette Square is the oldest neighborhood in DC, so we may think of its residences as being fixed and well established, but many have changed over time and
Ashburton House is no exception. When the Ashburton House was built in 1836,
it wasn't supposed to look much like the building you see today. Matthew St. Clair
Clarke, a clerk for the House of Representatives in the early nineteenth century, conceived his stately new home as a Greek Revival structure with a portico of ionic

marble columns at the entrance. Unfortunately, financial difficulties forced Clarke to give up the house shortly after it was completed and sell his marble columns, which today can be seen on the front of the historic Enoch Pratt House in Baltimore.

Though Clarke no longer owned the property, he was among a number of people who rented the house from its new owner in subsequent years. The most famous tenant was the house's namesake, Alexander Baring, First Lord Ashburton. For 10 months, he used the property to negotiate with Secretary of State Daniel Webster about US boundaries and criminal extradition. The result was the famous Webster–Ashburton Treaty, signed at the house on August 9, 1842, which settled US boundary disputes in the Great Lakes area and between the state of Maine and the province of New Brunswick. The ambiguity of the borders established in the Treaty of Paris after the American Revolution had caused a number of conflicts over the years. The most recent of these incidents was known as The Aroostook War, a confrontation that fortunately killed no one but raised plenty of issues.

In the years after the treaty, the house was owned briefly by William W. Corcoran, the philanthropist who founded the Corcoran Gallery of Art (another National Historic

Landmark), which was dissolved in 2014. Corcoran sold the house in 1853 to members of the Coleman/Freeman family, whose descendants owned the home for nearly a century.

In the 1850s after their purchase of the house, the family hired Thomas U. Walter to transform the structure into an Italian Palazzo style, meant to evoke the architecture of the Renaissance. Walter is probably best known for his work on the Capitol Building. He was the fourth Architect of the Capitol and designed the north and south wings, along with the iconic dome so associated with the building. In his work on the Ashburton House, Walter stuccoed the exterior and added stone window frames and iron cornices. In 1877, Walter returned to add another story and a mansard roof, thereby rendering Clarke's Greek Revival home unrecognizable.

The Coleman/Freeman family's decades-long residence at the house ended in 1947, when they sold it to the American Federation of Labor (AFL). The AFL converted the opulent interior of the Ashburton House to use as offices for its newly established League for Political Education. Not to be confused with a suffrage organization of the same name, the AFL's League for Political Education was created in reaction to the passage of the Taft–Hartley Act, which restricted union activities. The league's goal was to raise political consciousness in workers.

While the AFL sought to realize this goal, St. John's Episcopal Church, whose land was adjacent to the Ashburton House, had an interest in acquiring the property. In 1954, the church was finally able to purchase the house and gave the AFL its old Parish Hall, Rectory, and some of its property as part of the deal. The AFL used the land to build its new national headquarters after its merger with the Congress of Industrial Organizations (CIO). Meanwhile, the Ashburton House currently serves as the Parish House for St. John's.

Blair House
1651 Pennsylvania Ave. NW, Washington, DC 20503;
blairhouse.org; Closed to Public

Few buildings represent the history of diplomacy in DC like the Blair House. In its more recent life, this posh house has welcomed every president since Andrew Jackson and housed president-elects and visiting dignitaries. But there is more to this house than meets the eye. What began as an ordinary rowhouse in the president's neighborhood expanded over the years to include three neighboring townhomes, and today the compound is bigger than the White House itself. Though the building is just a short walk from the White House, it hasn't always served as the executive guest house.

The federal sand-covered limestone house was built in 1824 for the army's surgeon Dr. Joseph Lovell. The house's name comes from its second owner, however. During Andrew Jackson's presidency, Francis Preston Blair, a Kentuckian circuit court clerk and newspaper editor, drew the attention of one of Jackson's aides. Blair moved his family to DC in 1830 at the behest of Jackson's administration to take over the floundering *Globe* and make it into a pro-Jackson newspaper. He bought the house in 1837.

Blair became part of Jackson's "Kitchen Cabinet" and reported on many of Jackson's often controversial decisions as president, regarding the National Bank, the forced removal of Native Americans, and the like. In this sense, long before the house served a diplomatic purpose, its residents were painting the country and its president in a positive light. Because of his political activities during and after the Jackson presidency, the house entertained some of the most prominent figures of the nineteenth century including Daniel Webster, John C. Calhoun, and Henry Clay.

The Blairs moved briefly to Maryland, during which time Thomas Ewing, who was at various times Senator, Treasury Secretary, and the first Secretary of the Interior, took up residence in the house. Ewing is also known as the foster father to William Tecumseh Sherman, and Ewing's daughter Ellen married Sherman within the walls of Blair House in 1850.

When the Blairs moved back in the 1850s, the house expanded a bit after Francis Preston Blair's own daughter Elizabeth married Samuel Phillips Lee (yes, from that Lee family), and her father built them an adjoining house that began to be used as an extension of the original house; thus the building is sometimes known as the Blair Lee House.

There is another more notorious Lee connection, however. It was within the Blair House in 1861 that Robert E. Lee first announced his intention to refuse President Lincoln's invitation to command the Union Army. The Blair family may seem a strange choice to deliver this invitation, considering their past affiliation with the Democratic Party, but after the Kansas–Nebraska Act, their allegiances shifted. Blair's elder son, Francis Preston Blair Jr., a General and Congressman, fought to prevent Missouri from being roped into the secessionist movement. His other son, Montgomery Blair, was Lincoln's trusted advisor and postmaster general who lived in the Blair House for a time and made several additions and renovations.

Even with this illustrious past, the house nearly faced demolition in the early twentieth century as plans to modernize the capital abounded. The last of the Blairs to live there continued to redecorate and to entertain sitting presidents, but it was not until 1934 that the house, still at risk for development, became permanently preserved.

After witnessing Winston Churchill wandering the White House halls in nothing but a nightshirt in 1942, First Lady Eleanor Roosevelt saw a need for a guest house, and the house across the street seemed a perfect option. In the midst of World War II, foreign diplomacy was crucial, and so the long tradition of foreign leaders staying at the Blair House began.

When the White House underwent renovations during Harry Truman's presidency, the Blair House became his temporary residence. It was a site for cabinet meetings and the place where the Marshall Plan and the Truman Doctrine originated. It

was here that the decisions that led to US involvement in the Korean War were made and where Truman decided to fire General MacArthur. The most infamous event that transpired here during his presidency was an assassination attempt outside the front steps by members of a Puerto Rican Nationalist group. Today, a plaque commemorates a police officer who lost his life defending Truman that day in 1950.

Over the years, the house gained status not only for its many notable guests but also as a National Historic Landmark. More adjoining rowhouses were added to the compound in later decades to accommodate important meetings and visitors. The house, which has been altered and redecorated by various presidential administrations, still welcomes each president-elect before the inauguration. Though it still functions as a site of diplomacy and not a museum, within its walls are countless mementos testifying to its historic past.

Cleveland Abbe House
Arts Club of Washington, 2017 I St. NW, Washington, DC 20006; (202) 331-7282; artsclubofwashington.org; Open Tues through Sat; Free Admission

Like many historic houses in Washington, DC, this Federal-style townhouse has a history that extends far beyond its eponym. In addition to the famed meteorologist for which it was named, it has boasted many other residents, including a US president.

It is sometimes known as the Timothy Caldwell House, after the man who in 1808 purchased and completed the brick structure you see today. Construction began in 1802. Gideon Granger, US Postmaster, lived there for a time, but it was

Caldwell who apparently oversaw most of the construction of the elegant three-story Flemish Bond house in the Federal style of the new country.

Some (including the Arts Club that currently inhabits it) refer to it as "the Monroe House." In 1811, it was leased by none other than James Monroe, who moved to DC as President Madison's Secretary of State (and later his Secretary of War) and possibly stayed there through part of the 1814 British invasion. Because of the

destruction inflicted on the White House, the Caldwell House was also a temporary Presidential residence after Monroe's election, as he waited for repairs on the Executive Mansion to be completed. He and his wife hosted a postinaugural celebration there. It is likely that he brought some of the enslaved women from his Virginia plantation with him to keep house during his tenure at the Caldwell House, though their names are not recorded.

Following his departure to the White House, the British Legation (representing that country's government) rented the house until 1831, continuing the structure's role as a social center of DC. Later tenants included several diplomats, future Union General Silas Casey, and the owner of a boardinghouse, until the Caldwells finally sold the property to a State Department official in 1840.

It was not until 1877 that the house was purchased by the man whose name it currently bears. Professor Cleveland Abbe (who ironically started his career in Cincinnati) is known as America's first weatherman. When the US Weather Bureau was founded in 1871, Abbe came to DC to direct it. He broke ground in weather predictions by using technology (like the telegraph) to communicate with a team across a wide area to collect meteorological data for more accurate weather reports. A year later in 1872, he founded the *Monthly Weather Review*, a scientific meteorological journal that is still published today.

Arts Club of Washington Theater

Abbe moved into this house in 1877 and lived there until 1909. As a federal employee and a DC resident, Abbe used his influence to promote greater acceptance of science amongst the public. Following his death in 1916, his family sold the home to support the arts—to the Arts Club of Washington, to be specific. Inspired by similar clubs in New York and London, the institution formed in 1916 to promote visual, musical, and performing arts. Its first president, Henry K. Bush-Brown, sculpted many of the equestrian statues that stand today at Gettysburg. Unlike its predecessors, it was open to both men and women and attracted artists of all genres, including F. Scott Fitzgerald, Claudette Colbert, Tallulah Bankhead, and D. W. Griffith (best known as the director of the controversial film *Birth of a Nation*). It expanded by purchasing the adjoining house (former home of Brigadier General Robert MacFeely) in 1929 and hosted fashionable events into the 1960s. A 1963 fire led to the renovation of the building you see today, but the relatively stable ownership by the Arts Club has led to its protection and preservation. Today, the site functions as an art gallery for the club and also hosts events. Private tours are available on advance request.

Constitution Hall
1776 D St. NW, Washington, DC 20006; (202) 628-1776; dar.org; Open Mon through Sat; Closed to Visitors Except for Ticketed Events

The city block that most people think of as Constitution Hall is actually three distinct buildings that make up the headquarters of the Daughters of the American Revolution (DAR). The two other buildings in the compound are Memorial Continental Hall, facing 17th Street (see separate entry), and the DAR Administration Building in the center. Constitution Hall is the imposing Classical Revival building facing 18th Street.

John Russell Pope, the architect behind other DC buildings such as the Jefferson Memorial, the National Archives and Records Administration, the West Wing of the National Gallery of Art, and Meridian House (near Meridian Hill/Malcolm X Park, see separate entry), was responsible for designing the concert venue. Construction began on Constitution Hall in 1928, when First Lady Grace Coolidge laid the cornerstone. It was completed in 1929.

The DAR was founded in 1890 for female descendants of soldiers in the American Revolution. Constitution Hall was originally intended as a space for DAR's annual convention, but it became a very popular venue, the largest concert hall in the Nation's Capital. Over the years it has hosted cultural performances, TV shows, comedians, political debates, graduations, and events of all kinds. Every US president since Calvin Coolidge has attended some event or concert in the space.

One notable performance was by Washington DC's National Symphony Orchestra (NSO), which made its official debut there in 1930 and played to a very enthusiastic crowd. DAR's Constitution Hall was home to the NSO for another 41 years.

An infamous episode in the history of Constitution Hall was its rejection of Marian Anderson in 1939, when members of the DAR denied the famous opera singer the opportunity to perform there because of the color of her skin. Instead, she sang on the steps of the Lincoln Memorial on Easter Sunday, before an integrated crowd of 75,000 people, not to mention radio listeners. The iconic performance, which lasted just 25 minutes, has lived on in popular memory and Civil Rights History.

Part of the political impact of Anderson's concert was rising public pressure for the DAR to integrate its concerts at Constitution Hall. Anderson was eventually invited to perform at Constitution Hall in 1943 before an integrated audience, including two Supreme Court Justices and first Lady Eleanor Roosevelt (who gave up her membership of the DAR until it changed its racist policies). The color ban at Constitution Hall was not universally lifted, however, until 1952. Anderson performed there three more times throughout her career, including on the opening night of her farewell tour in 1964. The DAR has since apologized for its past actions of intolerance and amended the National Historic Landmark nomination for Constitution Hall to include Marian Anderson's story as part of the building's significance.

Historic interior of Constitution Hall

Today, the compound houses a genealogical library, an archive with an extensive Americana Collection, and a museum of the decorative arts, which has an entrance on D Street. While Constitution Hall is only open for ticketed events, take in its imposing facade and be sure to head around the corner to Memorial Continental Hall.

Decatur House
748 Jackson Pl NW, Washington, DC 20006; (202) 218-4333; whitehousehistory.org/the-historic-decatur-house; House Open Mon; Gift Shop open Mon through Fri; Free Admission

The Decatur House, the first private home in Lafayette Square, has a long and rather melancholy history. The first owners were the house's namesakes, Commodore Stephen Decatur and his wife, Susan, who commissioned the house from Benjamin Latrobe (who also worked on the Capitol, the White House, and St. John's Church, see separate entries) in 1816. Commodore Decatur was something of a celebrity for his naval heroics in the War of 1812 and Barbary Wars, and by the time the house was completed in 1819, it was one of the most fashionable in DC and ready to entertain members of Washington's high society. The Decatur House is the only one of Latrobe's residential homes still standing in the District, and the social standing of his patrons is evident in the house's design. The Flemish Bond brickwork on the exterior, with bricks laid at right angles to one another so that the shorter edge alternates with the longer edge, costs a pretty penny. Perhaps the strangest aspect of the house is its blind windows on the H Street side, which Latrobe conceived to mask a complex system of chimney flues. Inside, however, nothing looked amiss; with an elegant entry hall to welcome guests and an ample wine cellar in the basement, the interior of the house was designed with lavish parties in mind.

This legacy of partying continued as long as the house was lived in. From the 1870s on, the Beale family (the house's last owners who bequeathed it to the National Trust for Historic Preservation in 1956) continued the earlier tradition of diplomatic soirees within, adding their own Victorian flair to Latrobe's exterior (these touches were removed when the house was restored).

Though they started an entertaining tradition, a tragic event caused the Decaturs to leave the house after they'd lived there for just over a year. Over the course of

Commodore Decatur's illustrious naval career, he'd made an enemy of Commodore James Barron by voting against him as a judge in Barron's court martial hearing and accusing him of avoiding service in the War of 1812. Barron challenged him to a duel, and unfortunately, both men's "seconds," the people they chose to negotiate on their behalf, were also not too fond of Decatur and set the terms to his disadvantage. Both Barron and Decatur were hit in the fight, but only Decatur died from his wounds, reconciling with Barron before taking his last breath.

Susan Decatur could no longer bear to live in the home she had shared with her husband. She moved to Georgetown, refused to attend any party where Barron or either of the seconds were present, and rented her house in Lafayette Square to many notable figures, including Martin Van Buren and Henry Clay. This is where another ugly part of the house's history begins: its strong ties to slavery in DC. In 1829, Charlotte Dupuy, a woman enslaved by then–Secretary of State Henry Clay, sued him for her and her children's freedom based on a promise from her previous owner. Clay was threatening to remove her family with him to rural Kentucky, and Dupuy did not wish to leave the active community of free and enslaved Black people she had found in the capital city. While she was allowed to stay in DC until the court ruled against her in 1830, it was another 10 years before she or her children gained their freedom.

When Susan Decatur sold the house in 1836, its new owner was John Gadsby, proprietor of a tavern in Alexandria and the National Hotel on Pennsylvania Avenue. He brought between 15 and 21 enslaved people with him. These individuals lived and worked in a 900-square-foot servants' quarters in the back of the house, though some also labored at Gadsby's hotel, and Gadsby may have held others there

A painting of the Decatur House circa 1822

until they were sold. Today, the names and experiences of the people who lived here are a crucial part of the interpretation of the house. In 2020, protesters spray painted slogans like "Why do we have to keep telling you Black Lives Matter?" on the back of the house, one of the oldest surviving slave quarters in the area, an act which the Decatur House Museum documented as an instance of historical intersection between past and present.

Since 2010, the White House Historical Association has operated the Decatur House as a historic site and a popular event space. Also inside is the David M. Rubenstein National Center for White House History, which provides resources for research and education on the executive mansion and surrounding area.

Franklin School
925 13th St. NW, Washington, DC 20005 (Entrance on K St.); (202) 931-3139; planetwordmuseum.org; Open Thurs through Sat; Free, Donation Suggested

Though free public education is widespread throughout the country today, it was not always a given, even in the nation's capital. Its foundations, based on rural models, existed in the early nineteenth century, but only for the very poor and not on a widespread basis.

After the Civil War, as the country was trying to rebuild, an initiative to create such a system in DC as a model for the rest of the country took off. The Franklin School, completed in 1869, was the first of nine buildings to house DC's new urban public schools. At first, plans for the school were kept a secret from neighborhood residents, who feared their property values would decline with the presence of a public school. Adolf Cluss, the architect of the Smithsonian Arts and Industries Building (see separate entry), designed the red-brick structure, inspired by a German style with rounded arches, along with six other District public schools. The interior is equally as impressive. Cluss created a light, airy space in the masonry structure. It is one of few National Historic Landmarks that also has interior landmark status.

The school is named for Benjamin Franklin, an early advocate for public schools in the US. Cluss made a space for his bust at the top of the building. As Franklin was also an inventor and innovator, it is perhaps fitting that on the roof of the building, in 1876, Alexander Graham Bell successfully tested the photophone to transmit sound by light waves (the basis for modern fiber optics; see Volta Bureau entry) on the roof of the building.

Though this was a great factor in the building's preservation, its years as an educational space contributed greatly to its significance. The school's initial success worked to help change perceptions of public schools. It had an innovative curriculum that included music and arts, and also began to serve other functions tangential to its original purpose. For example, in 1880, the structure housed the first designated high school in the District. The Board of Trustees (later the DC Board of Education) was also located there, and would-be teachers studied at a normal school and gained hands-on experience with students within its walls.

The school's existence also serves as a reminder of a time when public schools would not allow all its students to mix. It was originally divided into two spaces: one for female and one for male students, each with separate entrances. African American students attended the completely separate Sumner school (also designed by Cluss and on the National Register of Historic Places) on 17th Street, which today serves as a museum and DC's public schools' archive.

In the twentieth century, as new schools were built to fill the growing demand for public education, the Franklin School gradually transitioned into Administrative offices by 1925. It was the official location for the DC Board of Education from 1928 to 1968. Like so many historic landmarks, it was nearly demolished after the city no longer saw any purpose for it. But there was public outcry over the possible destruction of the school which was once viewed with skepticism by the community. It received landmark status in 1996 and for a time served as a homeless shelter, which the DC mayor controversially closed in 2008.

Though the interior and exterior were legally preserved (though a bit dilapidated) at that time, a controversy arose in 2018 when developers hired to prepare the building to open as a museum removed some of the protected interior fabric,

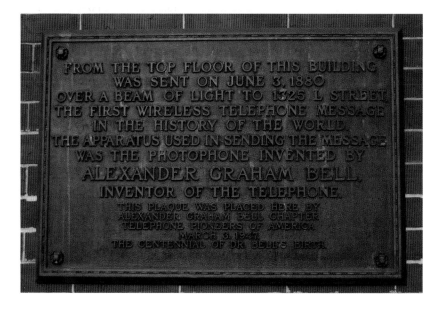

destroying wooden paneling and tin ceilings. DC officials investigated this egregious mistake, and the museum "Planet Word" opened in 2020. The museum features interactive, language-based activities, hearkening back to the original educational purpose of the space it exists in.

Lafayette Square Historic District
H St. between 15th and 17th Sts. NW, Washington, DC 20001;
Open Daily; Free to Public

No ordinary neighborhood, Lafayette Square may seem like an extension of the White House grounds, as it encompasses the land and buildings which surround it. Though it was at one point conceived as a "President's Park" in L'Enfant's plans, the space has a history beyond its relationship to executive power. It has historically been a space of power and influence, both by local elites and protestors.

Lafayette Park was used at various points as a graveyard, racetrack, open air market, and even a zoo. Due to its proximity to the Decatur House (see separate entry) which had strong ties to the slave trade, there is some historical speculation that the trade happened here as well.

Following the American Revolution, it quickly became the President's Park and site of staging for the White House construction. It was a space for encampment during the War of 1812 and a construction site again following the destruction of that war. With the president in town, it soon became a fashionable and influential neighborhood. Once Pennsylvania Avenue separated the "President's Park" from the White House in 1804, it became less for the president and more for the surrounding public. This separation became even more official 20 years later, when it was renamed in preparation for the Marquis de Lafayette's final visit to the US.

As more people moved into the area to gain political influence, more changes came for the park. Landscape architect Andrew Jackson Downing designed radial brick paths leading to Clark Mills's bronze equestrian statue of Andrew Jackson, interspersed with native tree plantings. The Civil War delayed major landscaping until 1872, but Jackson's statue, the first to be bronze cast in the US, went up in 1853.

An influx of elites came in during the postbellum era as the Nation was rebuilding from its crisis, including banker and art collector William Wilson Corcoran, and

Lafayette statue

descendent of two presidents, historian Henry Brooks Adams, who famously wrote of his neighborhood, "Beyond the Square, the country began." Thus, more adornments were added over the decades, including four statues of foreign Revolutionary War heroes at the corners of the park: General Marquis Gilbert de Lafayette (of course), Major General Comte Jean de Rochambeau, General Tadeusz Kościuszko, and Major General Baron Frederich Wilhelm von Steuben.

In addition to rich residents, new businesses and cultural institutions began popping up in the area in the post–Civil War era, such as the Freedman's Savings Bank, the Hay-Adams Hotel, the Cosmos Club, and the Belasco Theater.

As the Square moved into the twentieth century, it became increasingly less residential, with the final homeowner passing away during the Great Depression, perhaps representing a rise in the political power of groups and corporations rather than individual movers and shakers.

Though there were some landscaping changes in 1936, the economic crisis and World War II, along with its decline as a residential neighborhood, left it with an uncertain future. By 1954, the only home left was the Decatur House, and plans for modern office buildings threatened the whole Square with destruction. Upon Kennedy's election, First Lady Jacqueline Kennedy took steps to prevent this wide-scale demolition and preserve the entire Square as a historic site. Though many federal

Andrew Jackson statue

agencies do occupy the buildings around the White House today, the Square has been a National Historic Landmark since 1970.

Many gatherings and protests have historically taken place here, but the site became even more a part of the national consciousness in this regard with the weeks of demonstrations in the wake of George Floyd's death in 2020. Lafayette Square was a center of controversy as protesters attempted to take down the statue

A bronze statue of General von Steuben

of Andrew Jackson and some later questioned the tactics used by police to clear the Square.

If you visit today, you'll note that many of the buildings encompassed in this historic district are also listed individually as National Historic Landmarks. No matter where you turn in this neighborhood, you'll be face to face with a site of important events in our nation's history.

Memorial Continental Hall
1776 D St. NW (17th St., between C and D Sts. NW); (202) 628-1776; dar.org/national-society/about-dar/national-headquarters#memconhall; Open Mon through Sat; Free Admission

Though Constitution Hall is probably the most well-known and recognized of the DAR's buildings, Memorial Continental Hall, with an entrance on 17th Street, is the oldest of the structures in their complex and has a rich history in its own right. The Classical Revival building, with its large marble columns and grand porticos, opened in 1905. Its designer, Edward Pearce Casey, worked on several other high-profile projects in DC, including the Library of Congress interior, Taft Bridge over Rock Creek, and the Ulysses S. Grant Memorial on the National Mall. He won a national contest to design a structure which properly reflected the Revolution-era heritage that is so important to the DAR. The portico on the south side of the building, for example, has 13 columns, with the name of an original American colony carved on each base. Because of its structural similarity to the White House, several movies and TV shows, including *National Treasure* and *The West Wing*, have been filmed here.

Though today the DAR compound has a prime location within the city of Washington, when DAR leaders were looking for a place to build their headquarters in the late nineteenth and early twentieth centuries, they were unsure about the Foggy Bottom area. This part of the city was then a marshy and industrial landscape, and DAR leaders wondered if it would be suitable. In 1902, Senator James McMillan, mastermind of the McMillan Plan for DC (which echoed Pierre Charles L'Enfant's eighteenth-century design of grand vistas and wide streets), reassured them that this area would feature prominently in the city's future.

At the time of its construction, the DAR intended Memorial Continental Hall as a fireproof, all-purpose headquarters to store collections and hold meetings, events, and office space. The DAR held its annual Continental Congresses there, and in 1921 and 1922, the grand auditorium (today the library) hosted the Conference on the Limitation of Armament. These important negotiations ended with an agreement between the US, the British Empire, France, Italy, and Japan, though a number of other nations were represented there as well. The first arms limitations treaty ever signed, it essentially arranged to deescalate the race among these countries for superior naval technology after World War I.

During World War II, the Hall played another significant role, when the DAR lent its offices to the Red Cross and housed a War Service Center, which was open to those who were serving in the conflict.

As the DAR grew and the Administrative building (between Memorial Continental Hall and Constitution Hall) was constructed, the functions of Memorial Continental Hall changed. Its offices transitioned to the new building, and the DAR moved its library collections to the auditorium within the Hall.

Memorial Continental Hall's 31 offices, no longer needed, were given over to states. Each state selected was allowed to design a period-accurate interior, so that a walk through the Hall is a showcase of American styles of furnishing and decor in different regions of the country over different time periods.

Today, you can explore this museum of decorative arts with a self-guided or docent-led tour or do research on your family in the genealogical library.

The Octagon House
1799 New York Ave. NW, Washington, DC 20006; (202) 626-7439; architectsfoundation.org/octagon-museum; Open Thurs through Sat; Free Admission, Donations Suggested

There's more to the Octagon House than meets the eye. For example, most people think of the White House (see separate entry) as the main presidential residence in DC, but for a time, the Octagon House served that purpose. The house is also not octagonal. It has six irregular sides, but at the time it was completed in 1801, the term "octagon" frequently referred to shapes with eight angles, or rooms that were round but framed by eight sides.

This ambiguously shaped structure began as the winter home for John Tayloe III, one of the wealthiest Virginian plantation owners of his day and a slaveholder, who built his vacation house in DC at the recommendation of his friend George Washington. Tayloe hired William Thornton, first Architect of the Capitol, to design the house. Enslaved people from Tayloe's plantation likely contributed to the Octagon House's construction.

Tayloe had traveled extensively in Europe and encountered new architectural styles which influenced his vision for the house. Thornton incorporated these influences in a break from previous American architectural styles, like Georgian, which featured a perfectly symmetrical rectangular facade. The Octagon House, in its interior and exterior, includes several shapes but few unnecessary embellishments.

Perhaps because of its location near the White House, the Octagon House, like its neighbors, was a social center of the city. The Tayloes held many events during their stay there, but they were not the only residents. When the British burned the White House in 1814, the Tayloes offered their oddly shaped home to James and Dolley Madison for six months. Fittingly, President Madison effectively ended the War of 1812 in the house when he signed the Treaty of Ghent in a circular room on the second floor (today known as the "Treaty Room") in December of 1815.

The Madisons left, in part because their servants and slaves had become ill in the damp basement where they slept. In 1818, when the Tayloe family took up the Octagon House as a more permanent residence, they brought with them 12 to 20 enslaved people who lived and worked there. Specifically, the basement, soundproofed from the rest of the house, contained the kitchen and was their primary workspace. Their living quarters were in a building in the yard. The house was equipped with a system of bells to summon people (similar to the one at Monticello) and secret enclosed service stairways and waiting areas where servants could stay out of sight until needed. Historians know of at least one enslaved family, the Jacksons, who were separated, with parents Harry and Winney being brought to work at the Octagon house with their son Henry while the two daughters remained at the Tayloes' plantation in Virginia.

Tayloe also lived in the house with several of his 15 children. Two of his daughters are rumored to haunt the property; one purportedly died on the elaborate spiral staircase. Tayloe himself died in 1828. The family remained there until his wife's death in 1855, at which point they rented out the house and it began to serve new purposes. The neighborhood of Foggy Bottom was changing during this time, becoming more industrial and filling up with factories and breweries, which might have contributed to the wealthy and prominent Tayloe family's absence during this time. They leased the home to a Catholic girls' school, then (like so many DC buildings) as offices for the federal government.

Despite the changes that went on around it, the fact of the Octagon House's architectural uniqueness led to its preservation and ultimate destiny. In 1898, the American Institute of Architects (AIA), a professional association for the craft founded in 1857, began renting the house and purchased it in 1902. It became their headquarters until 1970, 10 years after it became a National Historic Landmark, when the AIA moved to a larger building behind it and opened the house as a museum.

Because of the architectural interests of the house's owners, there were several attempts over the twentieth century to remove the changes made over the years to the roof and other aspects and to restore the house to its original flat-roofed appearance. What you see today is, in theory, true to the house's original design and construction.

Today, the Octagon House is operated by the Architects Foundation (a philanthropic partner of the AIA) as a house museum, event space, and site for programs on the importance and role of architecture in society.

Side view of the Octagon House

Renwick Gallery
1661 Pennsylvania Ave. NW, Washington, DC 20006; (202) 633-7970; americanart.si.edu/visit/renwick; Open Daily; Free Admission

In its earliest years, the Renwick Gallery had a tumultuous history and served many purposes. But that was not the original intent of the building's designers and patron. The gallery is actually the first space in the entire US that was purpose-built as an art museum and is sometimes known as the "American Louvre."

William W. Corcoran, a DC native and successful banker, art collector, and philanthropist, commissioned the structure to house his vast collection of art (which eventually moved to his eponymous gallery on 17th Street, another National Historic Landmark). Architect James Renwick Jr. had already worked on another DC exhibit space, the Smithsonian Castle. Corcoran's goal for the building was to establish the US as a nation of arts and culture with a museum centered at its capital. Renwick therefore took his inspiration from the newest edition of one of the premier institutions in Europe at that time: The Louvre. From the mansard roofs, to the pavilions, to the paired pilasters which line the side of the building, there are many similarities to the "Second Empire Style" that was popular in France at the time. The Renwick

Gallery was one of the first such architectural specimens in the US and played a part in Second Empire's popularization in this country.

Construction began in 1859, but before the museum was even completed, the US was in the midst of a Civil War. Corcoran was a southern sympathizer, and so, in 1861, he moved to Paris, and the US Army seized the museum building to use as storage for the Quarter Master General's Corps. Union General Montgomery Meigs repurposed the building as his headquarters in 1864.

America's Louvre did not officially serve as an art gallery until 1874, after Corcoran had returned to the States, petitioned for the building's return, and established a museum charter. That iteration of the museum only remained there until 1897; the collection grew too big for the space, hence the move to 17th Street. Today, the National Historic Landmark on 17th Street is a school of art and design for George Washington University, and much of the collection is at one of American University's museums.

Like so many DC buildings, the federal government eventually purchased it, turning it over for use by the US Court of Claims. However, neither the building's beauty nor its federal use could guarantee its protection and preservation. It became dilapidated by the mid-twentieth century, when it was a popular trend to demolish older buildings and construct larger, newer government spaces.

First Lady Jacqueline Kennedy led a campaign in 1962 to preserve the building, as part of her larger goals for Lafayette Square (see separate entry). She was

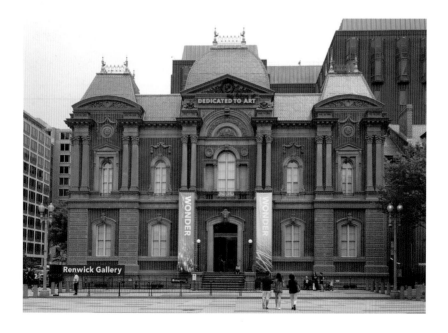

successful, and in 1965, the building found a new use (quite similar to its original purpose), when the Smithsonian Secretary S. Dillon Ripley asked President Johnson if the institution could use it as a museum. Once restoration of the structure was complete, it reopened in 1972. It once housed the 1903 Wright Flyer, Dorothy's Ruby Slippers, and the Hope Diamond, though they have since found different Smithsonian homes. At the time of the museum's founding, a revival was taking place in crafting, leading to the formation of an American Studio Craft Movement. Today, the museum often features works by craft artists in this tradition.

Interior stair, Renwick Gallery

St. John's Episcopal Church
1525 H St. NW, Washington, DC 20005; (202) 347-8766; stjohns-dc.org; Open Daily, Church Services Occur Regularly, But Visitors Are Welcome; Free Admission

With its closeness to the White House, St. John's is known as the "church of presidents" and for good reason. Every commander in chief since James

Madison has attended at least one service there since the church was established in 1815.

It was Madison who brought the church's architect, Benjamin Henry Latrobe, to DC in 1815, though not to design St. John's. Latrobe was called to Washington to oversee the restoration of buildings damaged by the British military invasion in 1814, including the White House and the US Capitol. St. John's Church was his first private commission in DC, though he is also responsible for designing the gate at the Navy Yard and the Decatur House (see separate entries). Latrobe arranged the church's floor plan in the shape of a Greek Cross, with all four arms of equal length and a central pulpit visible from all sides (the transept was later extended into the shape of a Latin Cross in 1820). Latrobe was also technically the church's first organist; on the day that St. John's was consecrated, he played a dedication hymn that he composed himself.

By 1816, the same year of the first service, the church formed a committee to offer then US President Madison a pew, which he insisted on paying regular fees for. That same pew (today numbered pew 54) has been reserved for all US presidents since. One president who made particularly good use of the pew was Abraham Lincoln. Although he officially belonged to a local Presbyterian church, he was often known to sneak into evening service at St. John's and leave unnoticed before it ended. Because of this well-known habit, the church was featured in the 2012 film *Lincoln*.

Some of the stained-glass windows at St. John's are dedicated to members of Lincoln's staff, including Secretary of State William Seward, General Winfield

Scott, and Postmaster General Montgomery Blair. There are also several presidents memorialized in the windows, many of which were replaced in 1883 with Lorin glass from Chartres, France. This style of stained glass, which is said to resemble oil paintings, represents a very distinctive period of nineteenth-century window design. It contains many neoclassical motifs, including stylized columns and borders surrounding biblical figures.

Also note the "Revere bell" in the steeple, which was cast by Paul Revere's son Joseph in 1822 and has been in continuous use (at times as a church bell and an alarm bell) since its installation. The project of installing the bell was overseen by the church's second rector Reverend William Hawley. He was known for frequently

The "President's Pew"

attending to the spiritual needs of DC's African American community, both free and enslaved. Many marriages and baptisms took place at his home near the church during his tenure, between 1817 and 1845.

Although the number of African American congregation members had dwindled to zero by 1960, St. John's showed solidarity with the Civil Rights Movement by hosting a special prayer service on August 28, 1963, the day of the March on Washington for Jobs and Freedom and Dr. Martin Luther King Jr.'s famous "I Have a Dream Speech." The service was open to all and was meant to encourage other denominations to support the marchers.

The church served as a site of Civil Rights debates again in 2020, when protests occurred directly outside its walls in the wake of George Floyd's death. A newer part of the church, including a nursery and part of the basement, was burned by protesters over the course of several days of demonstrations. During this tumultuous time,

the "church of presidents" served as the site of President Trump's controversial Bible photo op following the removal of protesters in Lafayette Square.

Today, the church is still in operation and holds services daily. Free guided tours are given after the last service each Sunday morning.

State, War, and Navy Building
(Old Executive Office Building) Eisenhower Executive Office Building, 1650 Pennsylvania Ave. NW, Washington, DC 20502; whitehouse.gov/about-the-white-house/eisenhower-executive-office-building; Closed to Public

Built on the other side of the White House (see separate entry) as a complement to the Treasury Building (see separate entry), the State, War, and Navy Building could not be more different from its counterpart.

Alfred B. Mullett, a supervising architect of the neoclassical Treasury Building, chose a much more elaborate style when he began designing the office space. The French, Second Empire architecture, much ridiculed when the building was first constructed (from 1871 until 1888), today serves as a model of the optimism and grandeur epitomized in postwar Victorian structures. Then the largest office building in the city, with its prominent mansard roofs, two miles of white-tiled corridors (Richard von Ezdorf, the interior designer, was inspired by actual Austrian and

German palaces), and the first federal building with an elevator designed prior to construction, was surprisingly born out of necessity.

The three departments it was built to house—State, War, and Navy—were all outgrowing their previous spaces as the government expanded over the course of the nineteenth century. The departments, in close quarters with the executive branch due to their influence on foreign policy, moved in gradually as the offices were under construction. Perhaps it's no coincidence that the US had much greater involvement in foreign wars in the ensuing decades.

Over the years, many future presidents held offices there: Teddy Roosevelt and later Franklin Delano Roosevelt, both as Assistant Secretary of the Navy, and Taft as Secretary of State. Hoover used an office there temporarily after a White House fire, as did Truman during construction on the White House (incidentally, Truman referred to the space as "the greatest monstrosity in America"). Countless secretaries of Navy, War, and State have also worked within these walls. Foreign representatives have also visited, including Winston Churchill and, after the bombing of Pearl Harbor, a group of Japanese emissaries.

As they continued to expand, the three agencies that called this building home slowly left for greener pastures (or rather, larger, newer office spaces—you can't get more beautiful space than some of the rooms in this building): first, the Navy Department in 1918, then the War Department in 1938, and finally the State Department in 1947.

While these larger departments transitioned out, new executive offices came in, including the Office of Management and Budget, the White House Office, the National Security Council, and the Office of the Vice President beginning in 1960. The latter, of course, resulted in many more future presidents working here, including the building's current namesake since 1997, Eisenhower, as well as Johnson, Nixon (who actually had a "hideaway" office there during his presidency, which he preferred to the Oval Office), Ford, and George H. W. Bush.

Despite its ongoing history, in the early twentieth century, as planners worked to modernize and classicize the Nation's Capital, critics of the building threatened to remake its facade into a twin of the Treasury Building, but protests and a lack of funding in the Depression era largely halted these plans. In 1957, there were renewed efforts at demolition, which thankfully failed until the building could be declared a National Historic Landmark in 1969.

Today, the space still serves as offices for the growing White House staff. This means that the interior is closed to the public, though there is an excellent virtual tour of the space available on Google Arts and Culture, which includes such curiosities as a desk signed by each vice president that used it (pretty much every recent VP except Hubert Humphrey, as Johnson remained in the office after Kennedy's assassination), the Secretary of War Suite, and the building's ornate library.

Treasury Building
1500 Pennsylvania Ave., NW Washington, DC 20220; (202) 622-2000; home.treasury.gov/services/tours-and-library/tours-of-the-historic-treasury-building; Tours Available upon Request; Free Admission

Though we may not think of it as an icon of Washington, DC, the US Treasury Building is something we may see daily—on the $10 bill. It may not be at the forefront of our national consciousness like the Capitol or the White House (see separate entries), but the operations of the Treasury Building were critical to the founding and day-to-day operations of the US.

Aside from the Capitol and the White House, the Treasury Building was the largest construction project in the nation's capital in the early nineteenth century. The original brick structure, one of the first federal buildings erected in DC, was completed by 1800. Unfortunately, the imposing structure (though small compared to the present-day offices) caught fire three times: in 1801, in 1814 during the British invasion of the Capitol, and again in 1833. In this case, the third time was certainly not a charm; the only part of the building to survive the blaze was a vault extension designed by Benjamin Latrobe in the early 1800s, which managed to survive the 1814 fire as well. Still, the government gave up on rebuilding the original structure yet again.

In 1836, Congress authorized a new building to be designed by Robert Mills, a former apprentice of Latrobe and architect of the Washington Monument and Patent Office (see separate entry). The most prominent aspect of his design is the colonnade spanning the east side of the building in a Greek revival style that could not outrival the nearby White House. Drawing from the Temple of Diana, it had thirty 36-foot-tall Aquia Creek sandstone columns, later painted white and eventually replaced with solid granite during a 1908 renovation.

In 1838, before Mills's design was even completed, some people, including Architect of the Capitol Thomas U. Walter, wanted to demolish it. The construction was proving costly, and Walter was brought on to take over the project from Mills in 1851 and make a few alterations, though several other architects would later succeed him before the building's completion, most notable of which was Alfred B. Mullett, who supervised construction from 1866 to 1874. Construction stalled again during the Civil War, when the carpenters' attention turned to building fortifications along the Potomac River and the building's south courtyard served as a site of encampment for Union soldiers.

Following Lincoln's assassination in 1865, President Andrew Johnson took up temporary residence there, receiving foreign ambassadors and issuing a warrant for Jefferson Davis's arrest from his offices in the Treasury Building. After the Civil War, the site served even more civic functions outside the realm of the Treasury, hosting Grant's inaugural reception in the elaborate Cash Room in 1869.

The Treasury Building, like so many federal structures, modernized and expanded in the late nineteenth and early twentieth centuries. New technologies were gradually incorporated into the existing structure (even concrete reinforcements and blackout shades during World War II) and a separate annex constructed across the street in the World War I era to accommodate the growing Internal Revenue Service (IRS).

In the 1920s, in tribute to two of the earliest Secretaries of the Treasury, a statue of Alexander Hamilton was dedicated and another, of Albert Gallatin, was

commissioned for the outside of the building. It was in 1927 that the image of the Treasury Building was first used on $10 bills, just two years before the start of the nation's most famous financial panic.

The Treasury Building received landmark status in 1972, not only for the important function it housed but also because it was practically the original template for countless office buildings (especially those built by the federal government). Though the building still serves its original purposes, visitors are allowed inside to see such highlights as the burglar-proof vault, the suite where Salmon P. Chase (Treasury Secretary during the Civil War) kept his offices, and the room used for hosting diplomats and important meetings. You can register for a tour online with your Congressional Office, but be prepared to bring some form of identification with you, as the Treasury takes security seriously.

The White House
1600 Pennsylvania Ave. NW, Washington, DC 20500; (202) 456-1111; whitehouse.gov; Tours Available upon Request; Free Admission

Arguably the most recognizable home in the country, every president except George Washington has resided at the White House. Yet, it was this first president who chose the site for the executive mansion in 1791 on a hill overlooking the Potomac River, as a critical point in L'Enfant's plans for DC.

Irish architect James Hoban designed the structure after winning a contest with his neoclassical plans, and construction began in 1792. Local carpenters and masons, as well as unskilled workers, worked on the project, including many enslaved people and white and Black wage laborers. The trademark white paint on the finished project initially served the purpose of protecting the stone on the finished walls from freezing and later became a stylistic choice as the home gained its nickname (which became official in 1901).

It quickly became a home, a center of government affairs, and a site of meet and greets and celebrations for the earliest presidents. But the first iteration of the White House didn't last long. In 1814, the British attacked the nation's capital and partially destroyed the symbolic center of the relatively new nation by burning down the president's house.

While President Madison and his family escaped, Dolley Madison famously had the presence of mind to save the silver, valuable papers, and a portrait of George Washington by Gilbert Stuart, entrusting their safekeeping to a gardener, steward, and enslaved manservant.

After the War of 1812 was over, Hoban returned to the project for its reconstruction (though the scars of the fire can still be seen on certain parts of the house) until President James Monroe took up residence there in 1817. The north and south porticoes were added to the building in the ensuing years. Still, by the Civil War, as the executive branch expanded, the house became too crowded to adequately serve its governmental purposes. Inaugural celebrations became so cramped that by Grover Cleveland's presidency, they spilled out into the streets in the form of the

parade that we're familiar with today. Though additions were considered, it wasn't until Teddy Roosevelt's presidency, in 1902, that renovations were made, the west wing was constructed and the executive offices relocated there (they were previously on the second floor). Taft's administration then arranged for the Oval Office to be added specifically for the president.

The renovations of the Teddy Roosevelt years only lasted so long. By Truman's presidency, the White House was falling apart. The changes made in this era were probably more significant than after the 1814 fire, with wholesale interior demolitions in some portions of the White House. Almost all the historic interiors everywhere but the third floor were rebuilt from scratch between 1948 and 1952, with a few new additions like the first version of the famous presidential bowling alley.

A decade later, First Lady Jacqueline Kennedy oversaw another interior restoration almost immediately after moving in, including collecting furniture and décor. Her alterations focused on different periods in the house's history rather than freezing the rooms in their earliest state of appearance. She founded the White House Historical Association in 1961 to publish a guide to the White House and oversee its programs. Though many presidents and first ladies have since made alterations to the house, the Kennedys' style of decoration and entertainment has been an inspiration for many of its modern residents.

Today, the White House is open for visitors—the only private home of a head of state that welcomes the public free of charge. Tours can be arranged in advance by contacting the office of your member of Congress. You won't be able to see every room if you visit, but you will be able to see several from Hoban's original design, including the Blue, Red, and Green Rooms, the State Dining Room, and a view of the Rose Garden. Each of these spaces in the president's home has served many functions over the years, so if you walk through the White House there will be a different history at every turn.

Healy Hall, see entry on page 88

GEORGETOWN

Georgetown Historic District
Bounded by Reservoir Rd. NW, and Dumbarton Oaks Park (North), Rock Creek Park (East), the Potomac River (South), and Glover-Archbold Pkwy. (West); georgetowndc.com/about; Open Daily; Admission to Buildings within This District Varies

While DC was built specifically to serve as a capital of a new nation, Georgetown is older not only than the capital city but the country itself. Originally part of Maryland, it was established in 1751 and named for King George II of England.

As a result, when you walk through the streets you'll see various styles of architecture dating from that time all the way up to today. The Old Stone House built in 1766 is the oldest surviving example of pre–Revolutionary War architecture in DC and is open today as a National Park Service site. Rows of townhouses from the nineteenth and twentieth centuries showcase the changing styles as Georgetown transitioned from a waterfront trading port reliant on tobacco (and to some extent, military supplies during the American Revolution) to the wealthy and gentrified neighborhood it is today. This was by no means a smooth or linear transition. Though Georgetown residents were initially eager for their city to be incorporated into the new capital, once it became part of DC in 1791 (as a separate jurisdictional entity until 1871) they faced new challenges such as lack of congressional representation, an issue which Marylanders did not have. On top of that, the new attention focused on the District of Columbia ended up detracting, rather than contributing to, Georgetown's shipping businesses. Still, Georgetown was at the center of the original thirteen states, and with its many waterways and the Patowmack Canal, and later C&O Canal, it was an important stop for international goods traveling North, South, and West.

As part of the new capital, Georgetown also faced an increased population. From its earliest days as a city, it was home to people of diverse religions, occupations, and ethnic backgrounds—leading to the establishment of a number of different churches, cemeteries, schools, and businesses. By 1800, around a third of the people who lived there were African Americans. Georgetown had a vibrant free Black population, which only expanded as the nineteenth century wore on. Many who escaped slavery stopped here along the Underground Railroad, and once the Emancipation

Proclamation allowed people to move north more freely, many newly freed people settled in Georgetown, particularly in Herring Hill.

In the late nineteenth century, a major flood damaged the C&O Canal, bankrupting the company behind it and beginning a period of economic hardship in Georgetown. Though it is prime real estate today, until the New Deal, when a renewed flow of government officials began moving into the neighborhood, its property values declined sharply.

Among those up-and-coming politicians to live here in the mid-twentieth century was John F. Kennedy, whose wife and children also lived there at various times (see Newton D. Baker House entry). Unfortunately, rising property values due to rising populations and even Georgetown's preservation as a historic district in 1967 gradually displaced many longtime residents. Today, it is still a popular home for government workers, a spot for shopping and tourism, in addition to the home of many college students at nearby Georgetown University (see Healy Hall entry). The area is full of cultural sites, like the stairs from the movie *The Exorcist* and the famous Blues Alley, where countless Jazz greats have played over the years. Grand mansions, like Dumbarton Oaks, Dumbarton House, Tudor Place (see separate

The Exorcist stairs

The Old Stone House

entry), and the Halcyon House, as well as historic churches and cemeteries are within its borders.

Though preserved as part of a National Historic Landmark, most of the buildings in the historic district are post-1870. As tempting as it is to think of Georgetown as a quaint part of the city frozen in time, it has been and continues to be in a state of constant change.

Healy Hall, Georgetown University
O St. NW & 37th St., Washington, DC 20007; (202) 687-0100; facilities.georgetown.edu/healy-hall; Building Closed to the Public

Probably the most recognizable building on Georgetown's campus, Healy Hall is named for the University's "second founder" Jesuit priest Patrick Francis Healy, who led Georgetown as president from 1874 to 1882. Healy's father was an Irish immigrant and plantation owner in Georgia, and his mother was formerly enslaved there. They married and sent their children, who were legally considered property in the state of Georgia, to the North to receive a proper education. Healy eventually went

on to earn his PhD in Europe and returned to his home country just after the end of the Civil War to teach Philosophy at Georgetown. When he became president several years later, he was the first person of African descent to head a university with mostly white students.

Healy fundraised and planned for the construction of his namesake academic hall in 1877, hiring J. L. Smithmeyer & Company, the architectural firm that designed the main building of the Library of Congress. Healy Hall, with its iconic 200-foot clock tower, was built in the ornate style of High Victorian Gothic; its steep gables and pointed arches are some of the most distinguishing features of this style. Local Potomac Bluestone, the material used as the foundation for many of the capital's earliest buildings, was used abundantly in its construction. President Healy, however, deliberately asked that the new hall face toward the District of Columbia rather than the Potomac River, to symbolize Georgetown's rise as a modern, national university.

The academic building was initially intended to house classrooms, laboratories, dormitories, a new library, and a meeting space for Georgetown alumni. Since it was constructed, however, some less-than-scholarly activities have taken place within its walls. It's a campus tradition for Georgetown undergraduates to sneak to the top floor of the tower to steal the hands of the clock every few years. In some of the more

interesting thefts, the pranksters supposedly sent the clock hands to the Vatican, to be blessed by Pope John Paul II. Another time, they were shipped to the White House, and the Secret Service dutifully returned them.

The two cannons in the front of the building also have quite a long and adventurous past. Their history may date as far back as 1588, when some theorize that these Spanish-made ordnances were discovered in a ship from the Spanish Armada after their loss to the British. When the first European settlers came to Maryland in 1634 (several Jesuits among them), legend has it that the cannons were on board their ships *The Ark* and *The Dove*, still capable of firing a nine-pound cannonball. While this part of their past is uncertain, the cannons were definitely part of Lord Baltimore's expedition to St. Mary's County in 1634 and stood guard in St. Mary's City and Fort Point later in the seventeenth century. Father James A. Doonan acquired the cannons during his tenure as president of the University. They were sent to Georgetown in 1888 and placed in front of Healy Hall 10 years later.

Today, Healy Hall houses administrative and academic offices, as well as the oldest library on campus and Gaston Hall, a historic venue for concerts, speeches, convocations and the like. As it is on a functioning college campus, the building is generally closed to the public, but visitors can schedule free tours of the school through the University Admissions Office.

Newton D. Baker House
3017 N. St. NW, Washington, DC 20007; historicsites.
dcpreservation.org/items/show/826; Closed to Public

When a private home in DC is as old as this one, chances are it has layers of significant history, private and public, political and otherwise. The Newton D. Baker House, for example, could be known by at least two other names—the Thomas Beall House and the Jacqueline Kennedy House.

The name Thomas Beall comes from the house's original owner, who constructed the stately brick mansion in 1794. He was the second mayor of Georgetown, a descendent of one of the powerful founding families of that area and a man with prominent political connections. His daughter married George Washington's nephew, and Beall himself oversaw the division of lots as DC was being established.

George Peter, one of Maryland's first congressmen, purchased the house after settling down from his service in the War of 1812. In addition to being a popular locale among politicians, Georgetown was an important spot for trade (see separate entry), and merchant John Laird, who had briefly lived in the house before, bought it in 1827. James Redin, the first auditor of the DC circuit court, was the next owner of the house, but it is possible that his daughter made the larger mark on it. There is some historical speculation that Catherine Redin turned the house over to a Ladies Seminary to educate the daughters of DC's prominent families. In any case, it was a private residence in 1890 when a man named John H. Smoot purchased it.

The official namesake of the house arrived on the scene in 1916 when he began renting the house from Colonel William E. Pattinson French. Newton D. Baker, the former mayor of Cleveland, Ohio, became confidante and war minister (Secretary

of War) to Woodrow Wilson and moved to Georgetown against the advice of his friends, who warned that the area was declining. Nonetheless, Baker, like so many federal employees, settled in Georgetown for the duration of his term in the president's cabinet, from 1916 to 1921. He was therefore responsible for quickly drafting and supplying an entire army when the US entered World War I. He was a great supporter of the League of Nations and a detractor of the idea of a "tomb of the unknown soldier," at Arlington, holding out hope that whatever unknown man was selected for the honor might later be identified. He continued to be active in the Democratic Party even after leaving DC.

After Baker, a string of military officials, ambassadors, and private citizens owned the house, modifying it and modernizing it with additions such as an elevator. First Lady Jacqueline Kennedy bought the house in 1964, after her husband's assassination the previous year. By moving to Georgetown with her children, she returned to the neighborhood where she and John F. Kennedy met in 1953 and where the two of them had lived after their marriage. What memories must have run through her head when the Warren Commission visited her at the Baker House to get her testimony about the assassination? She stayed in the house for only a year, then she moved her family to New York to get more privacy.

Later owners focused on restoring the house, which became a National Historic Landmark in 1976. Today, it is still a private residence within the Georgetown Historic District (see separate entry).

Tudor Place
1644 31st St. NW, Washington, DC 20007; (202) 965-0400; tudorplace.org; Tues through Sun, Feb through Dec; Free, Donations Encouraged

Tudor Place is in some ways a unique and remarkable historic site, where around 200 years of history are preserved and interpreted for visitors. This is mostly because the same family owned the property over several generations, from 1805 to 1983. Perhaps such careful efforts went into preserving the site's history because the first members of the Peter family to own it were Martha Parke Custis Peter (granddaughter of Martha Washington and step-granddaughter of George Washington) and her husband, Thomas.

The Peters first purchased the property in 1805. The house was not yet completed and consisted of only two wings of an unfinished structure left by the previous owner Francis Lowndes. In 1808, the Peters hired their friend William Thornton (designer of the Octagon House and handpicked by George Washington as first architect of the US Capitol; see separate entries) to complete the structure.

Thornton's plans united the two wings with other sections, with a domed temple portico as the house's centerpiece.

Martha and Thomas Peter lived in the house with servants, enslaved people, and their three daughters. Being staunch federalists, they named their children very national names, Columbia, America, and Britannia.

Britannia, the youngest, went on to own and care for the property for much of the nineteenth century. During the Civil War, she temporarily converted Tudor Place into a boarding house to avoid having it requisitioned and used as a hospital. Though many of her boarders were members of the Union Army, her own sympathies lay with the Confederacy, and she requested that none of the men who stayed there talk about the war in her presence.

Over the course of her long life (she died on the eve of her 96th birthday), Britannia managed the grounds, selling off a few acres of land, and cared for the incredible collection of objects associated with the house. These included original portraits of George Washington that had been gifted and left to his step-granddaughter, and furniture and objects that Britannia's parents purchased from Mount Vernon. When the Tudor Place estate was divided among Britannia's grandchildren after her death in 1911, these items and many more were carefully inventoried and labeled. Britannia and her relations had a huge role in curating the displays you see today, some stickers with numbers or the marking "Mount Vernon" can still be seen on objects like the plates in the dining room.

Eventually, Armistead Peter III inherited the property from his father, who had bought out the other grandchildren. Armistead carried on his great-grandmother's

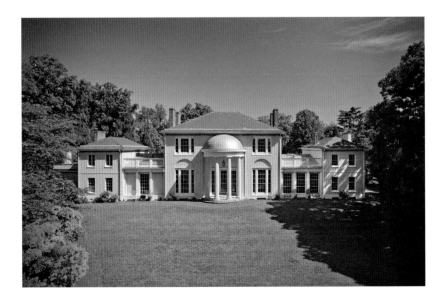

legacy of preservation. In 1966, he established a foundation to protect the house and open it to the public after his death.

Another interesting contribution he made to the property during his lifetime was the construction of an elaborate bomb shelter beneath the house. As a veteran of both world wars, Armistead prepared for possible nuclear destruction that might come with the Cold War in the 1960s. If you walk through the gardens, you can see a hatch to a passageway leading beneath the garage.

Also in the gardens are a Japanese Tea House, the oldest extant smokehouse in DC, and acres of carefully manicured landscaping. Inside the house, take a look at which items are currently on display. Tudor Place has a vast collection of documents and artifacts spanning centuries of history, including George Washington's camp stool from the American Revolution, a 1919 Pierce-Arrow Roadster, and a signed photograph of Woodrow Wilson. The guides also have a wealth of information about the servants and enslaved people who worked in the house.

Volta Bureau
3417 Volta Pl. NW, Washington, DC 20007; (202) 337-5220; agbell.org; Closed to Public

Alexander Graham Bell's invention of the telephone revolutionized the way hearing people throughout the world communicated with one another, but few people are aware of the direct connection between this invention and his work to advance the education of the deaf and hard of hearing.

Bell received a patent for the telephone in 1876 and moved to Washington, DC, a few years later with his wife, Mabel Hubbard, who had been deaf since her childhood (Bell's mother was deaf as well). In 1880, the French government awarded him the Volta Prize for his invention, an honor established by Napoleon in 1801 and named for Alessandro Volta, inventor of the electric battery and discoverer of methane.

Bell used the 50,000 francs he won to establish Volta Associates, a lab devoted to studying the recording and transmission of sound, in the carriage house on his parents' property in Georgetown. Along with his cousin Chichester Bell and inventor Charles Sumner Tainter, he worked on new inventions like the graphophone, which eventually became the Dictaphone; the photophone, a forerunner of modern fiber-optic telecommunications; and the induction balance, a sort of metal detector. Bell used the latter in an attempt to remove an assassin's bullet from President Garfield's body in 1881. Unfortunately, this attempt to save his life failed because the metal springs in Garfield's bed impacted the functioning of the machine. Still, Bell continued refining and inventing many new machines at the Volta laboratory, including a hearing test called the audiometer.

By 1887, Volta Associates had outgrown the space, and Bell used the profits from the patents he developed to found the Volta Bureau "for the increase and diffusion of knowledge relating to the Deaf." Its first location was his father's house, across the street from its current location.

Bell's philosophy of education was strongly tied to his father, Alexander Melville Bell, who invented a phonetic system called Visible Speech to allow deaf people to learn to talk. Unlike his contemporaries like Edward Miner Gallaudet, founder of Gallaudet University (see separate entry), Bell believed that lip reading and speech were a better option than American Sign Language (ASL) and thought that deaf students should not be separated from the hearing population.

The Volta Bureau worked closely with the American Association for the Promotion of the Teaching of Speech to the Deaf, founded in 1890, to achieve its goals. They eventually merged in 1908 and are today known as the Alexander Graham Bell Association for the Deaf and Hard of Hearing (AGBADHH), which still has its headquarters at the site. By 1893, the Bureau was developing new technologies and expanding, causing Bell to commission a separate building to house it.

The yellow sandstone building with its Corinthian columns stands out in Georgetown, which is not as replete with neoclassical architecture as the rest of DC. Twelve-year-old Helen Keller (who was connected by Bell to her tutor Anne Sullivan) actually broke ground on the building and came back for its re-dedication in 1950.

Bell published the *Volta Review* to publicize the institution, which initially housed a library collection of books on deafness. Today, it is one of the largest such collections in the world, and the *Volta Review* is still published by the AGBADHH. It still welcomes researchers on many topics related to deafness and works to promote education and access for people who are deaf and hard of hearing.

Meigs Vault at Washington Aqueduct, see entry on page 99

PALISADES

Washington Aqueduct
Washington, DC 20016; (202) 764-2753; nab.usace.army.mil/ Missions/Washington-Aqueduct; Portions Are Accessible to the Public; Free Admission

Most National Historic Landmarks in Washington are buildings, preserved for their architectural or historical importance, but a rare exception is the Washington Aqueduct, which supported the city and turned it into a modern capital. Though DC is, in some respects, meticulously planned with carefully thought-out streets and landmarks, its infrastructure is one area that remained relatively slapdash until well into the capital's history.

L'Enfant's plans identified Rock Creek as the city's main water supply, and in its infancy, when few people lived in the District and its landscape remained relatively undeveloped, this may have been enough. But as the city's population and construction began to boom in the nineteenth century, the lack of infrastructure became glaring in the face of increasing demand for water for drinking and fighting fires.

In 1851, a fire at the Library of Congress (see separate entry) was an impetus for change. The very next year, Army Corps of Engineers officer Montgomery Meigs (future Union Army Quartermaster General) conducted a survey of DC's needs, and in 1853 Congress allocated funds for one of the first aqueduct systems in the country.

Though DC recognizes the Aqueduct as a National Historic Landmark, much of it is actually in Maryland. Meigs believed the best source for the Aqueduct was the Potomac, and he conceived a dam to divert the water at one of the highpoints of the river, Great Falls (the original gatehouse is near the present-day C&O Canal National Park). From there, gravity would take its course across the more than 12 miles that the water needed to travel to reach DC. Gravity might seem like an obvious and simple means of transporting water, but the whole system was a lot more complicated than it sounds.

To facilitate the system, workers erected a sandstone gatehouse not far from the dam to control the flow of the water through a network of mostly underground conduits. In the areas where the water passed above ground, several bridges were built to travel across it, most famously the Union Arch Bridge across Cabin John Creek (a Historic Civil Engineering Landmark), which for a time was the longest masonry bridge in the world with just one arch. The water flowed into two reservoirs: the

Dalecarlia Reservoir, at the boundary between DC and Maryland, and the Georgetown Reservoir.

Water flowed into these reservoirs as early as 1863, but construction wasn't always an easy process. Issues with funding, workers catching malaria, and the advent of the Civil War were just a few of the extenuating problems the aqueduct project encountered. In a series of actions that echo current debates, two names inscribed on Cabin John Bridge, one of Meigs's assistant Alfred L. Rives and the other of former US Secretary of War Jefferson Davis, were removed after they allied themselves with the Confederacy (Teddy Roosevelt later replaced Davis's inscription).

Construction of the Aqueduct left lasting legacies beyond the final product. The dirt service roads that Meigs built to allow workers to construct the conduits contributed to DC's infrastructure once they were paved and renamed, first as Conduit Road and today known as MacArthur Boulevard.

Meigs was immensely proud of the project's outcome; he considered it one of his finest achievements and expected it to sustain the District's water supply for hundreds of years. Of course, as DC's population began to increase even more in the late nineteenth and early twentieth centuries, adjustments had to be made. A new reservoir near Howard University was added in the 1880s, and in the early twentieth century, with typhoid fever running rampant in the nation's capital, Senator James McMillan (of the famous McMillan plan for the National Mall) authorized a

A view from the Aqueduct dam

filtration plant to be built near Catholic University. Today, there are historic preservation efforts to save the filtration plant, which was phased out and replaced by other forms of water treatment. The Aqueduct, meanwhile, expanded over the course of the last century and is a wholesale water supplier to DC and parts of Northern Virginia, in addition to being a National Historic Landmark. This feat of engineering brought DC from its more rural, sparsely populated antebellum era status to its emergence as a more populous urban center supported by modern infrastructure.

Woodrow Wilson House, see entry on page 108

DUPONT CIRCLE AND KALORAMA

Anderson House
2118 Massachusetts Ave. NW Washington, DC 20008; (202) 785-2040; societyofthecincinnati.org/anderson_house; Open Tues through Sat, Library Mon through Fri; Free Admission

Contributing to the ritzy atmosphere of Dupont Circle is the impressive Anderson House. Larz Anderson—who over the course of his career served as second secretary at the US Legation to the Court of St. James's in London, first secretary at the US Embassy in Rome, US Minister to Belgium, and Ambassador to Japan—decided to make his home in this 50-room mansion.

Anderson and his wife, Isabel, commissioned the house from New England Architects Little & Browne. The Colonial revival mansion was completed in 1905, along with a tennis house, carriage house, stable, and gardens. As if it weren't luxurious enough already, the fact that the Andersons used their home only a few months out of the year made it seem even more so.

The house was custom-built to store their many valuables. The Andersons were art collectors of Asian art, tapestries, murals, and paintings, so certain walls throughout their mansion were sized to fit works of art. One such example is the large painting "The Triumph of the Dogaressa" on the landing of their staircase.

The elaborate design of the house perhaps reflected the Andersons' desire that Washington would grow into a capital as great as European cities. They invited prominent members of society and heads of state to the lavish parties hosted at the Anderson House, with guests like the Vanderbilts and Presidents Taft and Coolidge.

In 1937, following the death of her husband, Isabel Anderson gifted the house to the Society of Cincinnati to use as its headquarters. They moved in after lending the house briefly to the US Navy during World War II. Larz Anderson had been an active member of the Society of Cincinnati, which was established by officers in the American Revolution in 1783 with George Washington as its first President General. It was named for Lucius Quinctius Cincinnatus, an Ancient Roman statesman and military leader known for his civic virtue, and later gave its name to a well-known city in Ohio. Its initial purposes were to promote memory of the American Revolution and unity among the states and to maintain fraternal bonds between the descendants of its officers. Pierre L'Enfant, who planned the Nation's Capital, was

also responsible for designing the eagle insignia of the society. That eagle can be seen extensively throughout Anderson House, which has the largest collection of objects with that insignia in the entire world.

Today, in addition to serving as the headquarters for the Society of Cincinnati, Anderson House also is home of the American Revolution Institute, an advocacy organization to promote the legacy of this influential conflict through education and exhibitions. As a result, a library specializing in that period is available at the Anderson House to researchers who hope to study this era. In the museum portion of the house, visitors can see objects like portraits and weaponry from the Revolutionary era and Society of Cincinnati memorabilia, along with the furnishings and art collections of Larz and Isabel Anderson.

Carnegie Institution for Science
1530 P St. NW, Washington, DC 20005; (202) 387-6400; carnegiescience.edu/about/history; Closed to Public except for special events

DC is a political powerhouse, but few today think of it as an epicenter for scientific breakthroughs. It may come as a surprise then that Dupont Circle is the little-known headquarters of a research organization called the Carnegie Institution for Science.

Washington, DC, is relatively far from the steel mills of Pittsburgh, where Andrew Carnegie made most of his fortune, but this industrial titan and the philanthropy he engaged in had a very wide reach, which extended to the nation's capital.

In 1895, he allotted a significant portion of his riches to establish 23 organizations like public libraries and educational institutions. After his retirement in 1901, Carnegie at first wanted to establish a great university in Washington. Of course, DC already had several institutes of higher learning; most all of the well-known universities in the present day were established before 1900. To avoid competing with or diminishing existing schools, he instead founded a center for scientific research.

As the US capital, many prominent officials hoped that the city would become a locus of scientific development. As a result, when Carnegie endowed millions of dollars for the Carnegie Institution of Washington beginning in 1902, he chose President Teddy Roosevelt as well as other high-ranking politicians to be on the board of trustees. Thus, even this scientific organization was not out of reach from DC's political class; at its earliest meetings in 1902, it convened in the Secretary of State's office. The Institution was also in dialogue with some Washington staples of innovation and discovery; many board members had Smithsonian leadership roles.

Though not as flashy as some of its contemporary Smithsonian Museums (see separate entries), the Carnegie Institution is a Classical Revival, almost temple-like structure that fits right in with DC's most well-known government buildings. The columns inside and out gesture to the love of learning in Ancient Greece and give the building a sense of style in addition to function; it is a popular event space today. Carrère and Hastings, the same firm which planned the Carnegie-funded New York Public Library, was responsible for the building's design.

Even before the building was completed in 1910, however, research was already under way. The Institution granted fellowships to scientists and researchers in its earliest years but was soon divided into two sectors: Department of Terrestrial Magnetism (DTM), established in 1904, and the Geophysical Laboratory, established in 1905. These departments studied earth sciences and made a goal of mapping the earth's magnetic field. As technology and interests developed further in the ensuing decades, their focus grew to include the study of planets and fields like astronomy and astrophysics.

In 1937, the building was expanded and extra office space lent to scientists and scientific societies. During World War II, the National Defense Research Committee was established and housed here to scientifically advance warfare. One of the most famous advancements supported by the Institution in the postwar years was made by Barbara McClintock, whose discovery of "jumping genes" or transposable genetic elements won her the Nobel Prize. At the Carnegie-affiliated California observatories, Edwin Hubble made the revolutionary discovery of an expanding universe in 1919.

Understandably, with the many Carnegie-named organizations across the entire country, the research center took the name Carnegie Institution for Science in 2007

to avoid confusion with its affiliates in other states and with other Carnegie-named projects. Today, the research of its scientists spans the fields of earth and planetary sciences, astronomy, global ecology, plant biology, and developmental biology. Researchers are studying everything from the origins and development of life to the formation of our solar system.

Charlotte Forten Grimké House
1608 R St. NW, Washington, DC 20009; nps.gov/people/charlotte-forten-grimke.htm; Closed to public

As you walk past Dupont Circle's unique embassies and prominent mansions, this red-brick rowhouse might not immediately jump out at you. The writings of its most famous resident, Charlotte Forten Grimké, however, stand out today as a well-documented narrative of the life of this abolitionist, teacher, and women's rights advocate.

Forten Grimké kept a journal from age 16 and wrote intermittently throughout her life, including during her time in Washington, DC. Like many free Black intellectuals of her generation, she settled in the nation's capital after the Civil War. She initially moved there in the 1870s but spent only a few years of her residence there, from 1881 to 1886, living in the house that bears her name.

DC was by no means the only place she called home, however. She was very well-traveled throughout her life. Born in Philadelphia in 1837, her successful parents sent her to Salem, Massachusetts, at a young age to learn in integrated schools. It was at this point in her life that she joined the Salem Female Anti-Slavery Society and began her journaling. By the 1850s, she'd become a teacher and was active in publishing antislavery poetry, brushing shoulders with famed abolitionists like John Greenleaf Whittier and William Lloyd Garrison.

The most well-known entries in Forten Grimké's journals are from her time teaching on St. Helena Island in South Carolina at the Penn School, from 1862 to 1864. The first school in the South specifically for freed slaves, it was founded after Union Forces occupied the island in 1861 (and incidentally where Martin Luther King Jr.

stayed 100 years later to plan protests and marches). Forten Grimké's diaries from this period, published in *Atlantic Monthly*, reveal the stark differences she perceived between her life as a free, well-educated Black woman in the North and the lives of her formerly enslaved pupils. Documenting their growth and the struggles they faced was part of her advocacy for Black education and uplift, she happily wrote of their celebration when the Emancipation Proclamation officially ended slavery in the South.

After the war, she returned north and during her time in DC became very involved in local and governmental affairs. She taught African American students at the famous Dunbar High School and worked in the Treasury Department. It was also there that she married her husband, Rev. Francis James Grimké. Grimké, whose mother was enslaved and whose father hailed from a well-known southern family (his white aunts Sarah and Angelina famously moved north to fight for the cause of abolition), was pastor of the Fifteenth Street Presbyterian Church in Washington, a short walk from the couple's brick rowhouse on R Street.

Charlotte Forten Grimké assisted her husband in his ministry, all the while pursuing rights for women and African Americans. She helped found the National Association of Colored Women in 1896, as an alternative to white suffrage organizations that ignored the challenges unique to Black women, upholding and strengthening the rights of Black men in the face of laws passed to prevent them from voting was part of this strategy. Her commitment to social causes and civil rights, as well as to her writing and poetry, continued until her death in 1914. Today, her house is a private residence.

Woodrow Wilson House
2340 S St. NW, Washington, DC 20008; (202)-387-4062; woodrowwilsonhouse.org; Open Fri through Mon, Closed Weekdays in Jan; Admission Charged

"Embassy Row" in the Kalorama area of DC is one of the poshest places in the District, deriving its title from the many dignitaries, diplomats, and other international representatives who call it home. It is no surprise that a former president bought a house here in 1921.

The home in question is a red-brick Georgian Revival mansion, designed to mimic the architecture of the eighteenth and early nineteenth centuries. Waddy Butler Wood, the architect responsible for the Department of the Interior Headquarters, planned the home in 1915 for an executive at the Bigelow Carpet Company, Henry Parker Fairbanks.

Woodrow Wilson and his wife, Edith Bolling Galt Wilson, expected to build their dream house overlooking the Potomac once his third term ended—that's right,

Wilson was planning to run for an unprecedented third term in office. After Wilson suffered a stroke in 1919, his ensuing health problems threw a wrench in those plans. In fact, Edith Wilson is known by some historians as "the first female president" because of the strong role she played during his last year and a half of his second term, overseeing his affairs and hiding the fact that he was partially paralyzed and his vision impaired.

Edith fell in love with the property on Embassy Row, and President Wilson made her a gift of the deed to the house in December of 1920. Because the three-story mansion had some accessibility issues, the Wilsons added an elevator and a second-floor dining room and terrace (to access the outside world without descending stairs). They also expanded the library and added a billiard room. Woodrow and Edith Wilson

moved in on the last day of his presidency, March 4, 1921, the same day as Warren G. Harding's inauguration. Though he could not be present for the ceremony, Wilson's car ride escorting Harding to the event was one of his last public appearances.

Wilson received prominent company at his Kalorama home, however. The former prime ministers of Britain and France stayed there as guests, and Edith encouraged their friends to come over and read to the former president from one of the 8,000 books in his library. Though Wilson could not physically leave the house very often, he reached the people in other ways. He wrote an argument for foreign policy changes, published in August of 1923, and in November of that year he delivered a brief nationwide radio address for the fifth anniversary of Armistice Day. Wilson died just three months later, on February 3, 1924, at home in his bedroom.

His wife, Edith, kept the house's furnishings, as well as Wilson's many letters and commemorative objects from famous world leaders. She donated these items (including Wilson's cabinet-meeting chair, a mosaic from Pope Benedict XV, and many other artifacts of his presidency) to the National Trust for Historic Preservation. She continued living in this house until her death in 1961, curating her home as well as her husband's complex presidential legacy, which includes everything from delayed action on women's suffrage, to support of racial segregation in the US and the foundation of the League of Nations (precursor to the UN). The National Trust opened the house to the public in 1963 and has allowed visitors ever since.

If you choose to take the house tour, make sure to check out the backyard, which, like the house, was planned in a Georgian Revival style. It is the only known townhouse garden design by Waddy Butler Wood, with a variety of plants separated into four distinct sections of the yard. If you are viewing the house from the outside, take a look at its next-door neighbors. Another Waddy Butler Wood house is adjacent to Wilson's former residence, and at the end of the block is the former Textile Museum, designed by John Russell Pope (and recently occupied by Amazon and *Washington Post* mogul Jeff Bezos). Both buildings are on the National Register of Historic Places.

Carter G. Woodson House, see entry on page 113

LOGAN CIRCLE, SHAW, AND HOWARD UNIVERSITY

Carter G. Woodson House
1538 9th St. NW, Washington, DC 20001; (202) 426-5961; nps. gov/cawo/index.htm; Open Thurs through Sat; Free Admission (Fee Charged for Advance Reservation)

In the 1870s, city regulations allowed for more adventurous features in street architecture, like bay windows and molding that projected beyond the sidewalk. This brick Italianate rowhouse may have much fancier archways and molding than its peers in other neighborhoods, but it was rather restrained for its time and looks uniform compared to the others on its street. It was a long-standing boarding house before Woodson purchased it in 1922. But thanks to Carter Godwin Woodson, extraordinary things happened within its walls.

Born in Virginia, Woodson moved North in his youth, and in his twenties put himself through high school and college. He eventually became the first Black man with formerly enslaved parents to earn his PhD. He came to DC in 1909 to work on his history dissertation, but he also taught at M Street and Armstrong public high schools and later went on to become head of graduate faculty and dean of Howard University's School of Liberal Arts. At a time when the ideology of white supremacy was on the rise, Woodson recognized the broader need for education in the African American community and for representation of Black people in history; he founded the Study of Negro Life and History, Inc., in 1915 and the associated journal *The Journal of Negro History* in 1916.

By the time Woodson moved to the rowhouse, he received grants that enabled him to work full time on these important projects. The basement and first floor of the house on 9th Street, then, became the headquarters for the association (today the Association for the Study of African American Life and History or ASALH), the journal (today the *Journal of African American History*), and eventually the *Negro History Bulletin* (today the *Black History Bulletin*), begun in 1937 to reach a wider audience. Woodson lived on the floors above these busy operations for nearly 30 years.

Woodson shared his space with other great minds of his generation, like Mary McLeod Bethune, who became the first female president of the ASALH in 1936 and served longer than anyone else. Langston Hughes assisted him there throughout the 1920s. Before Woodson's death in 1950, he welcomed countless African American students and scholars into the house to do research in the basement archives, which preserved documentation of the African diaspora and the experience of African Americans.

Though Woodson didn't live to see the establishment of Black History month in 1976, he laid the foundations for this commemorative time of learning and reflection half a century earlier. In 1926, in his "office-home," Woodson masterminded the first "Negro History Week," in the month of February, situated near President Lincoln's and Frederick Douglass's birthdays.

Unfortunately, the significance of Woodson's legacy as it pertained to this house was forgotten for many years after the ASALH left in 1971. Though the National Trust designated it a National Historic Landmark five years later, the house remained

vacant and fell into extreme disrepair before the National Park Service bought the property in 2005.

The house that you visit today has been restored to its appearance during the era of use by Woodson. After touring the house, stop by the nearby park, which also bears his name. There, a statue in his likeness sits on a concrete monument, seemingly waiting to engage in historical conversation with the passersby. In combination with the house where he lived and worked, this park and the statue of him commemorate the scholarly and social contributions he made not only to his city but also to the nation.

General Oliver Otis Howard House
Howard Hall, 2401 Sixth St. NW, Washington, DC 20059; nps.gov/
places/general-oliver-otis-howard-house.htm; Closed to Public

The General Oliver Otis Howard House (today Howard Hall) was not a government building, but its occupant played a crucial role in shaping the trajectory of the country's administration.

The house was finished in 1869, but Howard had already achieved a great deal by that point by serving as the head of the Bureau of Refugees, Freedmen, and Abandoned Lands (more commonly known as the Freedmen's Bureau) since 1865. His qualifications for this important post stemmed from his experience as a General in the Union Army. He lost his arm in the war and was known as "the Christian general" for his devout evangelical beliefs.

Heading the Freedmen's Bureau was a bit of an uphill climb. This was due in part to the nature of the organization, which was designed to provide humanitarian aid but affiliated with the Department of War with mostly soldiers as its initial employees. Howard clashed with President Andrew Johnson's more conservative attitude and his prioritization of patching things up with the South over helping newly freed African Americans.

Like Howard himself, the Bureau has a contested reputation today, with allegations of institutional corruption and ineffectiveness. Yet, under Howard's leadership, the Freedman's Bureau still managed to accomplish much in the way of integration, fighting against Black Codes passed by former Confederate States, and instituting policies of social and medical welfare, political organization (especially after the passage of the Fourteenth and Fifteenth Amendments), and educational programs. The latter area is where Howard devoted most of his attention, even as the Bureau lost funding in 1868 and shut down in 1872.

Along with a group of other white men, Howard helped to found his namesake university in 1867. They initially conceived it as a theological seminary, but it expanded to include law and medicine as well and became a university that welcomed students of any sex or skin color.

After the Civil War, as men like Howard attempted to reinvent the country, an architectural style called Second Empire fittingly rose to prominence in government buildings. A far cry from neoclassical federal buildings, this style, with Renaissance influences, derives its name from a French architectural movement under the Empire of Napoleon III. Second Empire is distinguished by mansard roofs, iron balconies, and the like. Rather than letting the university pay for his home, Howard purchased the lot himself, and once the house was completed in 1869, he served as Howard University's third president until 1873.

Howard went on to represent the US Army in Native American affairs, negotiating a treaty with the Chiricahua Apache in 1872, and later violently removing the

Nez Perce from Oregon as the commander of the Department of Columbia in that state. Upon Howard's death in 1909, the university purchased his former residence and surrounding property.

The building was one of the original structures on the Howard University campus and the only one to survive until the present day. It has served multiple purposes over the years, housing other faculty, the African Studies Department, and African Language Center, and in the present day it serves as a university event space.

Mary Church Terrell House
326 T St. NW, Washington, DC 20001; nps.gov/places/washington-dc-mary-church-terrell-house.htm; Closed to Public

As you walk past LeDroit Park Historic District's many pastel Victorian townhomes, the first thing that may strike you about this brick house is that it looks rather incomplete. Typical of the simplified Victorian style of home built in DC in the early twentieth century, a fire destroyed the other half of this duplex in the 1970s, but the sturdy brick firewall fortunately protected the home of an important leader in education, suffrage, and civil rights. The house may look incomplete, but it marks a very full life.

Mary Church Terrell was born in 1863 to formerly enslaved parents who were prominent in Memphis's Black social circles. Her family's relative prosperity allowed her to pursue education, and she is known as one of the first African American women to obtain a college degree (at Oberlin College in Ohio) and even went on to get her master's. She arrived in DC in 1887 to teach at M Street High School. There she met fellow educator Robert Herberton Terrell, whom she eventually married.

At a time when schools in the District were still segregated, Mary Church Terrell served on the city's school board as the first Black woman in the country to hold such a position. She was a firm believer in racial uplift through education and tried during her tenure to make DC's school system a more equitable place for its Black students.

Outside of her job, she fought for equal rights as an active member of the National American Woman Suffrage Association (NAWSA). In 1896, she helped found the National Association of Colored Women (NACW), a federation of women's clubs that advocated for women's rights and uplift. She served as its first president until 1901 and established the organization's monthly newsletter. She was among the founders of the NAACP (among many other associations she played a role in founding) and actively promoted anti-lynching campaigns. In 1940, she published her autobiography, focused on her fight against discrimination, entitled *A Colored Woman in a White World*.

Though Mary Church Terrell did not live in her duplex until later in life, her activist days were by no means over. She and her husband fought segregation informally, by encouraging other influential African Americans to move to their neighborhood. Terrell also engaged in a formal battle against discrimination.

The District passed integration laws in the Reconstruction era, but these had long since been reversed, and by the mid-twentieth century, Jim Crow laws were still actively enforcing segregation in DC's public places. Terrell sought to change this in 1950 when she and a few others purposefully entered the John R. Thompson Restaurant, were denied service, and filed a lawsuit that went all the way to the Supreme Court. In the *District of Columbia vs. John R. Thompson Co.*, the Court ruled in 1953 that the Reconstruction-era laws, though long unenforced, were still in effect—and segregated restaurants in DC were unconstitutional. In her 80s, Terrell's involvement in the landmark court case paved the way for future Civil Rights victories like *Brown vs. The Board of Education*.

Terrell's house went vacant and neglected for years even after it was designated a National Historic Landmark, as neighborhood demographics continued to change and the significance of the house was overlooked. At one point, it was considered an "endangered" historic site, but today a campaign sponsored in part by its current owner Howard University (see separate entry) is working to restore it.

Mary Church Terrell House undergoing restorations

St. Luke's Episcopal Church
1514 15th St. NW, Washington, DC 20005; (202) 667-4394; st lukes.org; Open for Services and by Appointment; Free Admission

Washington in the post–Civil War years was a city in transition, especially for its African American population. What was to begin with a large and vibrant free Black population grew in size and autonomy during this time. It was in this period of the Reconstruction era that an African American Episcopal congregation known as St. Mary's Colored Mission, started by St. John's Church (see separate entry) in 1867, outgrew its meeting space on 23rd Street and decided to go its own way. This coincided with a larger trend during this time of free Blacks forming their own congregations in the southern US, now that their churches didn't require white supervision.

By 1879, Reverend Dr. Alexander Crummell had established a separate congregation for African American Episcopalians. Crummell was a very well-respected clergyman from New York who studied at Cambridge after being barred from an American Seminary because of his skin color. He served as a missionary in Liberia after his ordination, where he supported Black emigration for a time before moving back to the US.

Crummell was impressed with England during his studies, by the opportunities he encountered and by the education he received there. Crummell used his sway to encourage the new church, begun in 1876, to be constructed in an English Gothic style. Calvin T. S. Brent, widely known as the first African American licensed architect to practice in DC, was just 22 years old when he began designing the house of worship in collaboration with its first pastor. The young architect used relatively local materials in the angular facade, which is made of Chesapeake bluestone, but the church's European legacy is obvious in the gothic archways above its doors and elaborate stained-glass windows. The Early English Gothic style Crummell envisioned, however, wasn't quite as showy as later gothic churches with soaring pointed towers. It was much more horizontal, with cozy oak paneling inside rather than the celestial ceilings of French Gothic. The church itself was meant to represent the potential that it had to promote education and opportunities (like those Crummell received in England) for DC's Black population, and Brent designed it with this in mind.

Brent, whose father founded the John Wesley AME Zion Church in DC, went on to design several other religious spaces controlled by free Black people in the Nation's Capital, including Mount Jezreel Baptist, Third Baptist, and Miles Memorial Colored Methodist Episcopal Church, as well as many row houses in Northwest DC and near Capitol Hill.

Rev. Dr. Crummell, meanwhile, remained at St. Luke's long enough to see it through its earliest decades, not only overseeing the building of the church but also fundraising and recruiting a thriving congregation (he took it from 35 to 300 people). Shortly after leaving St. Luke's in the 1890s, he began to lecture about Civil Rights advocacy and founded the American Negro Academy in 1897, an intellectual group which encouraged African Americans to pursue education in the liberal arts, as opposed to vocational training for Black people promoted by figures like Booker T. Washington.

Prominent men such as W. E. B. DuBois (who vocally supported a classical education for African Americans) and poet Paul Laurence Dunbar were members of this group, designed to further liberate and uplift America's Black population.

The legacy Crummell left as first rector of the first Black Episcopal Church in Washington, DC, continued long after his tenure at St. Luke's. A number of capable

individuals succeeded him and served an active parish community in the twentieth century, with several notable members. DC native Edward W. Brooke, a coauthor of the Civil Rights Act of 1968 and the first Black Senator since the Reconstruction era, attended services at St. Luke's.

Over the years, the church has gained a reputation for its sense of community, its excellent choir music, and its openness to people of all backgrounds. If you visit, be aware that the church is still very much in use for Sunday morning services, which all are welcome to attend.

Twelfth Street YMCA Building
1816 12th St. NW, Washington, DC 20009; (202) 462-8314; tmcsh.org/about; Open Mon through Fri; Free Admission

In 1908, Teddy Roosevelt laid the cornerstone of this Italian Renaissance Revival building to house a branch of the Young Men's Christian Association (YMCA), but this was by no means the beginning of the history of this particular YMCA branch.

The first YMCA built for African American men came out of nearly half a century of efforts, primarily those of a remarkable man named Anthony Bowen.

Bowen was born into slavery in Prince George's County, Maryland, in 1809. He purchased his freedom in his mid-twenties and moved to DC. There, he became an educator and religious leader, founding the St. Paul AME Church out of his home (which was incidentally also an Underground Railroad stop) and establishing a school for free Blacks. He was also the first African American employee at the US Patent Office (see separate entry), where he met William Chauncey Langdon, founder of DC's YMCA, and learned more about the process of establishing a branch. The organization was founded in England in 1844 in response to new issues brought with urbanization and came to the US in 1851. It sought to build community among young men and offer them mental, physical, social, and religious development. Unfortunately, the YMCA did not extend this offer to young Black men, and the DC branch was closed to them.

Bowen pushed to change this, but faced opposition, and the organization itself refused to fund a YMCA for African Americans. Bowen nonetheless founded an unofficial "Colored Young Men's Christian Association" (which at the time functioned more as a club) in 1853 using his own money. The branch moved from space to space, never securing a permanent home due to limited funding. Through the Civil War and Reconstruction, Bowen continued to hold meetings, build community, and promote the freedom of African Americans in DC, though the YMCA struggled due to the extenuating obstacles people of color in DC faced once segregationist policies hindered their employment and social development. He died in 1872 and was succeeded by another leader, his mentee, Rev. James A. Handy, in 1866, who made a constitution to officially form the "Colored YMCA." By 1867, the YMCA had laid groundwork for the existence of "separate-but-equal" branches for Black men, although the DC branch was not officially incorporated until 1892. By 1900, there were branches in 21 cities throughout the country, but only six of these owned their own buildings.

After fundraising efforts, the YMCA was finally able to purchase a building on 11th Street in 1891 and moved to a space on U Street as membership fluctuated. The 12th Street structure was the first that was truly its own, built by and for Black men with enough space to accommodate growing membership, a swimming pool, a gymnasium, and dozens of boarding rooms. William Sidney Pittman, the architect (and Booker T. Washington's son-in-law), designed the Italianate structure in a style popular among contemporary white institutions, symbolizing the social aspirations and philosophical purposes of buildings like clubs and athletic facilities. At a time when many "separate-but-equal" facilities for Black people were grossly inadequate, Pittman created a dignified, state-of-the art space for the YMCA as a center of the local community. Many other African American YMCAs would follow its example of fundraising to secure their own spaces.

It supported men like Langston Hughes, who published his first works of poetry while staying there, and blood transfusion scientist Charles Drew. Even as it faced challenges of existing discrimination in the broader YMCA organization, and even as the once-vibrant neighborhood around it declined in the 1960s once segregation ended and people moved to integrated areas, the YMCA continued on in this space until 1982. In 1973, on its 120th anniversary, it was rededicated and renamed after its founder Anthony Bowen. After a period of vacancy, it was renovated in the 1990s to become the Thurgood Marshall Center for Heritage and Service to restore its position as a center of community and a focal point of the Shaw neighborhood. Today, the center includes exhibits on the building's past, event spaces, and offices for local initiatives. Call ahead if you're planning on bringing a large group to view the exhibit.

The Yard, Howard University
2441 and 2365 6th St. NW; and 500 Howard Place NW, Washington, DC; (202) 806-7275; howard.edu/about/history; Closed to the Public

Chartered by Congress in 1867, Howard University is one of the most famous and renowned Historically Black Universities in the country. It began as a theological school run by white men. Soon more disciplines and faculty joined the university, and by 1869 Black attorney and professor John Mercer Langston opened its School of Law, intended to help defend the rights of African Americans in the Reconstruction era. The landmarks at Howard are recognized as a place where students and professors at this powerful law school worked together to desegregate education in the US.

"The Yard" at Howard University is one of those National Historic Landmarks that encompass multiple sites. Three buildings in this grassy section of campus— the Andrew Rankin Memorial Chapel, Frederick Douglass Memorial Hall, and Founders Library—are all designated on the National Register of Historic Places. As Howard's campus grew from one building to the large university it is today, the Yard became a central hub for students going to classes and events. It may seem like a typical center of a prestigious college campus, but if you visit, you will walk past the buildings where Civil Rights attorneys studied, taught, and trained to fight legal injustices.

Among these was legal legend Charles H. Houston, special counsel to the NAACP beginning in 1935, who taught at Howard University from 1924 until his death in 1950. He helped Howard's law program become the first to gain accreditation at a Black university, and in 1936, he introduced the first Civil Rights course to be taught in an American law school at Howard.

Houston also worked closely to mentor one of the most famous legal minds to come out of Howard University. Though the vast majority of the plaintiff's attorneys in the 1954 landmark Supreme Court case, *Brown vs. The Board of Education*, were students or professors at Howard, future Supreme Court Justice Thurgood Marshall was by far the best known. The research and strategies that Marshall and the rest of the legal team used in the *Brown* case (as well as numerous future Civil Rights cases) came from the resources at Howard University. Many graduates of Howard Law School returned to practice test runs of their desegregation cases in the 1930s, 1940s, and 1950s. The critiques that they received from peers and professors in the law program paved the way for their success in landmark legal cases like *Brown*.

If you visit today, be aware that Howard University is an active college campus with students who continue to learn and worship on-site. Many of its buildings contain added areas of interest. Founders Library houses the University Museum, as well as the Moorland Springarn Research Center, Howard's center for the study of the Black experience. For those who wish to visit, tours of the campus are available by calling the University Admissions Office.

Andrew Rankin Memorial Chapel

One of the buildings contributing to this National Historic Landmark served the spiritual needs of law students at Howard. The Andrew Rankin Memorial Chapel,

From top to bottom, Rankin Memorial Chapel, Douglass Memorial Hall, and Founders Library

the oldest of the historic landmarks on the Yard, was finished in 1895 and named in memory of the brother of the university's president, Jeremiah Rankin. The red-brick towers, arches, and steep gables are typical of the Gothic Revival movement of the late nineteenth century. Inside, the first floor was initially an Art Gallery and later turned into the Howard Thurman Lounge, a center for religious activities. Upstairs is the sanctuary, where many Civil Rights icons and political figures have visited. The chapel hosts services for people of many different faiths in the present day, with notable speakers frequently coming to deliver sermons. As you enter the chapel, note the unique stained-glass windows. Many depict aspects of Howard's past, such as the "A Century of Worship and Service 1894–1994" window, which features likenesses of the chapel's former deans.

Founders Library

Next to the chapel is possibly the most iconic building on Howard's campus with its unmistakable clock tower, Founders Library. It was designed by Albert Cassell, an assistant professor in Howard's architecture department. Cassell planned the expansion of Howard University that took place in the 1930s, making it the hilltop campus so well known today. Founders Library, dedicated in 1939 to the founders of the university, was the last of Cassell's designs to be completed. From 1944 to 1955, the third floor of the building was home to the law school and its library.

Frederick Douglass Memorial Hall

Also among the many campus buildings Cassell designed was Frederick Douglass Memorial Hall finished in 1935. Douglass was an original member of Howard's Board of trustees, and the hall's large classical columns and portico once led into the departments of history, psychology, and education, as well as a number of administrative offices. The name of this academic hall, combined with its significance to Civil Rights battles, indicates the close link between nineteenth-century abolitionists, the founding of Howard University, and the legal minds that trained there.

Meridian Hill Park/Malcolm X Park, see entry on page 133

COLUMBIA HEIGHTS AND UPPER NORTHWEST

Mary Ann Shadd Cary House
1421 W St. NW, Washington, DC 20009; nps.gov/nr/travel/ underground/dc2.htm; Closed to Public

This unassuming Italianate brick rowhouse is part of the Greater U Street Historic District, a neighborhood that developed with the booming population and economy in the decades after the Civil War. In the twentieth century, it became a focal point of DC's African American community, but this house is most famous for its four-year resident Mary Ann Shadd Cary, who lived here from 1881 to 1885.

Despite her brief tenure there, the house's namesake was so prolific in her many endeavors, as a journalist, teacher, lawyer, and activist for the freedoms of African Americans and women, that her residence received due recognition as a National Historic Landmark in 1976.

Shadd Cary was born in Delaware in 1823 to free parents, who instilled in their daughter a passion for education and the cause of abolition. They even moved to Pennsylvania so that their children could attend school (Black schools were illegal in Delaware at that time), and Shadd Cary went on to teach African American children in Delaware, Pennsylvania, and New Jersey. Though she was born into a position of relative privilege compared to the many African American women in the US, in another sense, she saw her experience as a Black woman as typical and was vocal about the challenges like racism and sexism that she encountered in the North despite her education and social standing.

The Compromise of 1850 created a tense atmosphere in the northern US, with the passage of the Fugitive Slave Act, which mandated that escaped slaves be returned even if they were caught in a free state, included as part of the political bargain. Shadd Cary moved to Canada with her brother Isaac (whose house in Chatham ended up being the site of a secret convention in 1858 at which John Brown announced his famous raid on Harpers Ferry) in search of enhanced opportunities and a less racist society. In 1853, Shadd Cary founded Canada's first antislavery newspaper, the *Provincial Freeman*, and published several pamphlets that encouraged American Blacks to come to Canada. Yet, she was far from being a proponent of resettlement and was unafraid to criticize abolitionists, both white and Black, who encouraged African Americans to leave the US and establish colonies in places like Africa. She faced criticism from fellow abolitionists for giving Black women a bad reputation with her outspokenness and her vocal dislike of charity programs for Black refugees to Canada.

Shadd Cary returned to the US once the Civil War began to recruit for the Union Army and settled in Washington, DC, at the war's end. She began law school at Howard University (graduating in 1883) and continued teaching. She became an advocate for women's suffrage, the rights of emancipated Blacks (two causes frequently entwined in this era but ultimately divided by the Fifteenth Amendment allowing Black males to vote), and fought against racism and discrimination against Black women within the suffrage movement. She was one of 600 women to sign the National Woman

Suffrage Association's (NWSA) petition for women's legal right to vote and founded her own organization, the Colored Women's Progressive Franchise Association. In 1871, she unsuccessfully attempted to register to vote in a national election. By 1876, she wrote to white suffrage leaders at NWSA asking that they include the names of Black suffragists in DC on their centennial Declaration of the Rights of the Women of the US.

Shadd Cary's dogged activism as compared with some of her contemporary female abolitionists made her a controversial figure and one long overlooked by history. If you stop by her house, be sure to check out some of the numerous nearby sites in the U Street Corridor like The Lincoln Congregational Temple United Church of Christ, Howard Theater, and Whitelaw Hotel, to name a few.

Meridian Hill Park/Malcolm X Park
16th St. & W St. NW, Washington, DC 20009; nps.gov/places/meridian-hill-park; Open Daily; Free Admission

One of the best views of Washington, DC, can be seen from Meridian Hill Park, aka Malcolm X Park. The park's two names reflect efforts to erase and reclaim African American history of the site.

The name Meridian Hill Park, used at its opening in 1936, pointed to a century's history of land development in the area. In 1804, President Thomas Jefferson asked that an obelisk be placed to mark a point on one of the four meridians of Pierre Charles L'Enfant's original plan for the capital. The new marker lined up with a milestone marker that surveyors Benjamin Banneker and Andrew Ellicott placed at Jones Point, Virginia, in 1791 (it is among the points on the longitudinal White House meridian, which also includes points like the Zero Milestone and the Jefferson Memorial). In 1819, a wealthy man named John Porter built a mansion in the area and named his estate "Meridian Hill" in honor of its geometrical situation.

This homage to the Meridian Hill estate glossed over its history in the second half of the nineteenth century. President John Quincy Adams rented the mansion from the Porter Family after he left office. In 1861, the site was known as Camp Cameron. Union Troops requisitioned part of the estate, as well as adjoining land belonging to Columbia College (precursor to George Washington University) to use as an encampment. Once the war ended, a theological school for African American men called Wayland Seminary was established on the land of the estate.

It was not until several decades after the Civil War that the park took the shape you see today. In 1887, former Senator John Brooks Henderson and his wife, social reformer Mary Foote Henderson, moved into the neighborhood. They built a lavish mansion, "Boundary Castle" along 16th Street, and eventually acquired many other nearby plots as well. Mary Henderson pushed for more changes to the area, including a new executive mansion to be built at the crest of Meridian Hill, just across the street from her castle (she later wanted the Lincoln Memorial to be built near her home as well).

Though she didn't succeed in either of these schemes to raise property values, it was her vision that led to the creation of Meridian Hill Park. Congress authorized the purchase of land for the park in 1910, and the Department of the Interior hired a whole team of landscape architects, most notably George Burnap and Horace Peaslee, to design the layout and plantings in the style of Italian Renaissance gardens. The park officially opened in 1936.

Even before 1936, the space had many park-like markers, including several statues that remain to this day. One of the most controversial is of President James Buchanan, whose legacy of shaky leadership at the start of the Civil War and support of slavery won him few admirers among Republican congressmen in 1918 to the point that they tried to prevent the statue.

After World War I, when countless French soldiers carried her medal in battle, France gifted a statue of St. Jeanne d'Arc in 1922 (it is the twin of one that sits in front of the Cathedral of Notre Dame in Reims). Meridian Hill's Maid of Orleans unfortunately had her sword stolen in 1978, but it was replaced in 2011. She is the only statue of a woman on horseback in the entire District. You'll also see a sculpture of Dante and a memorial meant to depict "Serenity," and it's hard to miss the Renaissance-inspired cascading fountain, the largest of its kind in North America

Mary Foote Henderson's vision resulted in the beautifully landscaped park you see today, but its creation harmed neighborhood residents. Congress's purchase of the land evicted many working-class African Americans who had lived in a community of frame houses there since 1867. This was one of the instances of displacement of African Americans that continued throughout the century in projects termed "urban renewal."

In the 1960s, however, Black Power activists reclaimed the park as a popular meeting place. At a rally held there in 1969, political activist Angela Davis declared the park a symbol of Black Pride. By the end of the decade, it was unofficially known by locals as Malcolm X Park, despite unsuccessful efforts to officially change the name. Today, the park is known sometimes as one, the other, or both names.

If you're mulling over the park's activist history as you walk through it, here's some more food for thought: Fidel Castro made a stop here when he visited DC in 1959, just a few months after he took power in Cuba. There is plenty to see here, with frequent events and performances, most notably a weekly drum circle that meets at the park.

Buchanan statue

United States Soldiers' Home
140 Rock Creek Church Rd. NW, Washington, DC 20011; (202) 829-0436; lincolncottage.org; Open Daily; Admission Charged for Lincoln Cottage

Near the outskirts of Washington, DC, not too far from the McMillan Filtration Plant and very close to Catholic University and the National Shrine of the Immaculate Conception, is the Old Soldiers' Home or Armed Forces Retirement Home as it's known today. It is one of the largest National Historic Landmarks in the District, which overlooks much of the city and comprises six acres and several structures, including the eponymous Soldiers' Home and President Lincoln's Cottage.

The cottage that would become Lincoln's Camp David–esque retreat within the city started out as someone else's private getaway. The estate, formerly a plantation, was named "Corn Rigs" in the 1840s, referencing the "rigs" (Scottish for "furrow") and the crop that grew on the land. It may've also been a reference to the house and land's owner, wealthy banker George Washington Riggs. In 1851, the US government purchased his land and the Gothic Revival cottage for an "asylum" for army veterans. A similar institution already existed for the navy in Pennsylvania, which provided shelter and support to wounded and disabled retired military members. Future Union General Winfield Scott and future President of the Confederacy Jefferson Davis pushed for an army counterpart in DC.

In its earliest years, a number of Romanesque Revival buildings, quarters with rounded arches, and the Sherman Building with its majestic tower were constructed. The original Sherman Building, however, was modeled in great part after the Smithsonian Institution (see separate entry). Though later modifications like the mansard roof made it look downright Victorian, today it is restored to its castle-like appearance. The building was originally called Scott Hall, after the general who championed the Soldiers' Home's creation. In 1857, Winfield Scott offered the Soldiers' Home as a summer retreat for President Buchanan, who relaxed on-site in one of the quarters.

By 1862, another Commander in Chief, Abraham Lincoln, moved into the old Riggs Cottage with his family for the summers and falls of his presidency. In the midst of a Civil War, these were most certainly working vacations. Lincoln commuted to the White House daily for the majority of his stay, passing soldier and contraband encampments on the way, and used the cottage as a place to strategize and develop his position on Emancipation. He actually made an early draft of the Emancipation Proclamation here, and on September 22, 1862 (just days after the Battle of Antietam), he released an early version stating his intent to free Southern slaves the following January.

Though the Soldiers' Home was far away from the center of DC at that time, there were constant reminders of the surrounding city and the war for the Lincoln family, especially when they were sometimes evacuated to escape enemy fire. That didn't stop President Lincoln from going to the Soldiers' Home to watch the attack on Fort Stevens led by Confederate General Jubal Early, though.

Lincoln intended to return to his summer retreat in 1865, but never made it. After his assassination, his successor Andrew Johnson declined to use the cottage. Later presidents like Hayes and Arthur revived its use as an executive home but were the only others to do so.

In the years without a president, the cottage blended into the other functions of the Soldiers' Home as a hospital and a living quarters for residents and even employees. In 1889, it was renamed after another founder of the home, Union General Robert Anderson, the first governor of the Soldiers' Home (present at the start of the Civil War in Fort Sumter). It was not until the Soldiers' Home gained national monument status in 2000 that the presidential history of the site was again brought to the forefront.

Today, the cottage is open for visitors, and the rest of the site still serves as a home for members of the Armed Forces. Adjoining the site is the US Soldiers' and Airmen's Home National Cemetery, one of the oldest national burial grounds in the country which, like the Soldiers' Home, pays respect to veterans of multiple wars.

This statue acknowledges Lincoln's frequent presence at the cottage on the Soldiers' Home property

FRIEND
TEACHER
BENEFACTOR

Gallaudet Memorial, see entry on page 141

NOMA AND NEAR NORTHEAST

Gallaudet College Historic District

Florida Ave. between 6th and 9th Sts. NE, Washington, DC 20002; (202) 250-2474; gallaudet.edu/campus-design-and-planning; Open to Public; Free Admission

There are many historic universities in Washington, DC, but only Gallaudet University's campus has acres belonging to a historic district. Though it was ultimately selected as a National Historic Landmark for the significance of its architecture and landscape design, the college today is best known as a preeminent academic institution and resource for deaf and hearing-impaired people in the US and throughout the world. It is the only institution of higher education in the US specifically focused on deaf students.

The school had its beginnings in 1856, when lawyer, journalist, and Democrat politician Amos Kendall donated his home and two acres of his estate for the establishment of the Columbia Institution for the Education of the Deaf and Dumb and the Blind, which was chartered by Congress a year later.

Kendall chose Edward Miner Gallaudet, whose father established the first deaf school in the US, as the first superintendent of the institution. When the Columbia Institution transitioned into the National Deaf Mute College in 1864, he became its first president. The first graduates received diplomas signed by President Grant, and the tradition of presidential signatures on the diplomas of Gallaudet graduates continues to this day.

The original campus, which consisted of just a few buildings, was transformed two years later by the plans of Frederick Law Olmsted, the most famous American landscape architect of his generation who designed countless green spaces, including Central Park in New York.

Olmsted's design divided academic buildings and faculty residences (including Edward Miner Gallaudet's large Gothic Revival mansion) by a large, grassy area. His aim was to make the campus as visually pleasing and stimulating as possible for its hearing-impaired students. At the center, he suggested the placement of the college's central buildings. The first of these to be built was Chapel Hall, the High Victorian Gothic hub of the campus, in 1870, which included the dining hall, chapel, and auditorium. The weathervane atop it reads "IDD," Institution for the Deaf and

Dumb. The colorful, asymmetrical design is typical of post–Civil War romanticism in architecture, and Gallaudet specifically requested the brownstone building include touches like a clock tower to make the college stand out as a nationally significant institution. Note the patriotic eagle relief that embellishes the main roof gable.

You will also see several other imposing structures, the largest of which is the Victorian towered, red-brick College Hall, built in 1877 as a dormitory. Today, it houses the university's administrative offices. The red, gingerbread-looking Queen-Anne revival structure was originally a state-of-the-art gymnasium in 1881, but today serves as an alumni house.

Gallaudet remained the head of the college throughout all this construction and changes; he helped to grow the student body and was a fervent promoter of American Sign Language. In 1894, he renamed the school after his pioneering father, Thomas Hopkins Gallaudet, whose foundation of the American School for the Deaf in 1817 inspired his son's work.

Thomas Hopkins Gallaudet's statue, which sits across from Chapel Hall, depicts the story of his interaction with a deaf child, Alice Cogswell. This influential

Ballard House

College Hall

interaction led him to dedicate his life to teaching deaf and hearing-impaired children. The statue, sculpted by Daniel Chester French (who created the statue at the Lincoln Memorial), was a gift from the National Association of the Deaf in 1889.

Since then, the university has grown in size and prominence. In 2005, the ASL Deaf Studies Department collaborated with architect Hansel Baumen to create influential guidelines for what is known as the "DeafSpace" project. This approach focuses on promoting personal safety, visual language, and community building for deaf people experiencing the built environment. The project addressed "sensory reach," or spatial orientation; created space for individuals to maintain enough distance for visual communication during sign language conversations; and improved poor lighting and acoustics to limit the strain of eye fatigue and distraction of reverberations. The university has since incorporated this approach in some of its campus buildings.

If you visit, be sure to check out the National Deaf Life Museum in Chapel Hall, where you can schedule tours in advance by visiting the university website. Though Gallaudet University is an open campus that welcomes visitors, please be mindful that this is a space where students live and study.

The Gallaudet Memorial

Thematic Index

Invention and Innovation

Military History

Photo Credits

Wikimedia Commons/By The Norman B. Leventhal Map & Education Center at the Boston Public Library viii; Christopher M. Taylor/Getty Images xii; Wikimedia Commons/By Smallbones 2; Wikimedia Commons/By USCapitol 3; Wikimedia Commons/By Dmadeo 5, 50; Wikimedia Commons/By Smash the Iron Cage 6; Wikimedia Commons/By Hugaholic 7; Courtesy of the Marine Barracks in Southeast Washington, DC Collection, Library of Congress, Prints and Photographs Division 9 (top); Wikimedia Commons/By USMC Archives, from Quantico, USA 9 (bottom); Courtesy of the Historic American Buildings Survey Collection, Library of Congress, Prints and Photographs Division 10, 123; Wikimiedia Commons/By Ser Amantio di Nicolao 12, 52; Wikimedia Commons/By AgnosticPreachersKid 13, 28, 63, 64, 66, 75, 81, 96, 104, 107, 109, 117, 122, 125, 132, 134, 142, 143; Wikimedia Commons/By Jchandler69 15; Wikimedia Commons/By Sunira Moses 16 (top); Courtesy of the Harris & Ewing Collection, Library of Congress, Prints and Photographs Division 16 (bottom) 54; Wikimedia Commons/By dbking 18, 22, 87 (top); Wikimedia Commons/By Martin Falbisoner 19; Wikimedia Commons/By National Museum of the U.S. Navy 21; Flickr/By Onasill ~ Bill 24; Wikimedia Commons/By Matthew G. Bisanz 26; Wikimedia Commons/By Difference engine 30 (top), 46, 60; Wikimedia Commons/By Zack Frank, Smithsonian American Art Museum 30 (bottom); Wikimedia Commons/By Gryffindor 32 (top); Wikimedia Commons/By User:Kmf164 32 (bottom); Flickr/By BenFranske 34; Courtesy of the 1946 Carol M. Highsmith Archive, Library of Congress, Prints and Photographs Division 36, 148; Wikimedia Commons/By Antony-22 37; Wikimedia Commons/By MamaGeek 39 (top); Wikimedia Commons/By Jeremy Peschard 39 (bottom); Wikimedia Commons/By Kevin Burkett 41; Wikimedia Commons/By Ad Meskens 42; Wikimedia Commons/By Sarah Stierch 44; Wikimedia Commons/By Cliff 45; Wikimedia Commons/By Ben Schumin 49; Wikimedia Commons/By Daderot 51, 61; Wikimedia Commons/By Edna Barney from Virginia 55; Wikimedia Commons/By Slowking4 56, 135; Wikimedia Commons/By White House Historical Association 57; Wikimedia Commons/By Andy Mabbett 59; Wikimedia Commons/By David 62; Wikimedia Commons/By Steveturphotg 68, 69; Wikimedia Commons/By Tony Hisgett 70; Wikimedia Commons/By Another Believer 71, 72; Wikimedia Commons/By Jerrye & Roy Klotz, MD 73, 136; Wikimedia Commons/By Tim 1965 74; Wikimedia Commons/By Yuhan Zhang 76; Wikimedia Commons/By Dreamyshade 77; Wikimedia Commons/By Sealy j 80; Wikimedia Commons/By CC-BY-SA-3.0/Matt H. Wade at Wikipedia 82; chemistkane/Getty Images 84; Wikimedia Commons/By Dmitry K

Acknowledgments

My sincerest thanks to my editor Sarah Parke of Globe Pequot Press for entrusting me with such a rewarding project and for answering my questions and supporting me every step of the way. I also thank Dr. Whitney Martinko of Villanova University, who advised me as a first-time author and helped me to refine my approach to writing a book about Washington, DC. Special thanks to the staff of each and every one of these National Historic Landmarks that is open to the public for being so helpful and responsive to queries about visitor information. Especially as many of the sites temporarily closed because of the pandemic, their willingness to answer phone and email, or even to offer socially distanced assistance truly meant a lot. Thanks to Mark Jones and WETA for giving me my first opportunity to write about DC's local history. Thanks to Jane, for being just as excited about this book as I am, and to everyone who gave me opinions on photos. Finally, thanks to my Mom, Dad, Priscilla, and John for encouraging me, looking at my entries, and sharing their opinions on my work.

About the Author

Lori Wysong is a writer, researcher, editor, public historian, and museum professional. She is a graduate of Villanova University's MA program with a concentration in Public History, and an alumna of Washington College and Montgomery College. Her research interests focus on historic spaces and the built environment in various locations and time periods, including Barcelona at the turn of the twentieth century, Philadelphia in the nineteenth and twentieth centuries, and, of course, Washington, DC. Lori grew up in Maryland in a suburb of DC and Baltimore and frequently visited the District for both work and leisurely exploration. She has written for online publications like "Hidden City Philadelphia," WETA's "Boundary Stones" local history blog, the Lepage Center for History in the Public Interest's "Hindsights" blog, and Villanova's "Historically Speaking" blog. She also works at a historic site and has worked in the past at a National Park, a historic Customs House, and a Smithsonian museum (the National Portrait Gallery, to be specific). When she's not immersed in local history, she enjoys being outdoors, listening to her favorite music, and spending time with her family. She currently lives in Wayne, PA, and can be reached via LinkedIn.